DAVID

THE SHEPHERD'S SONG

VOLUME 1

CHAPTER 1

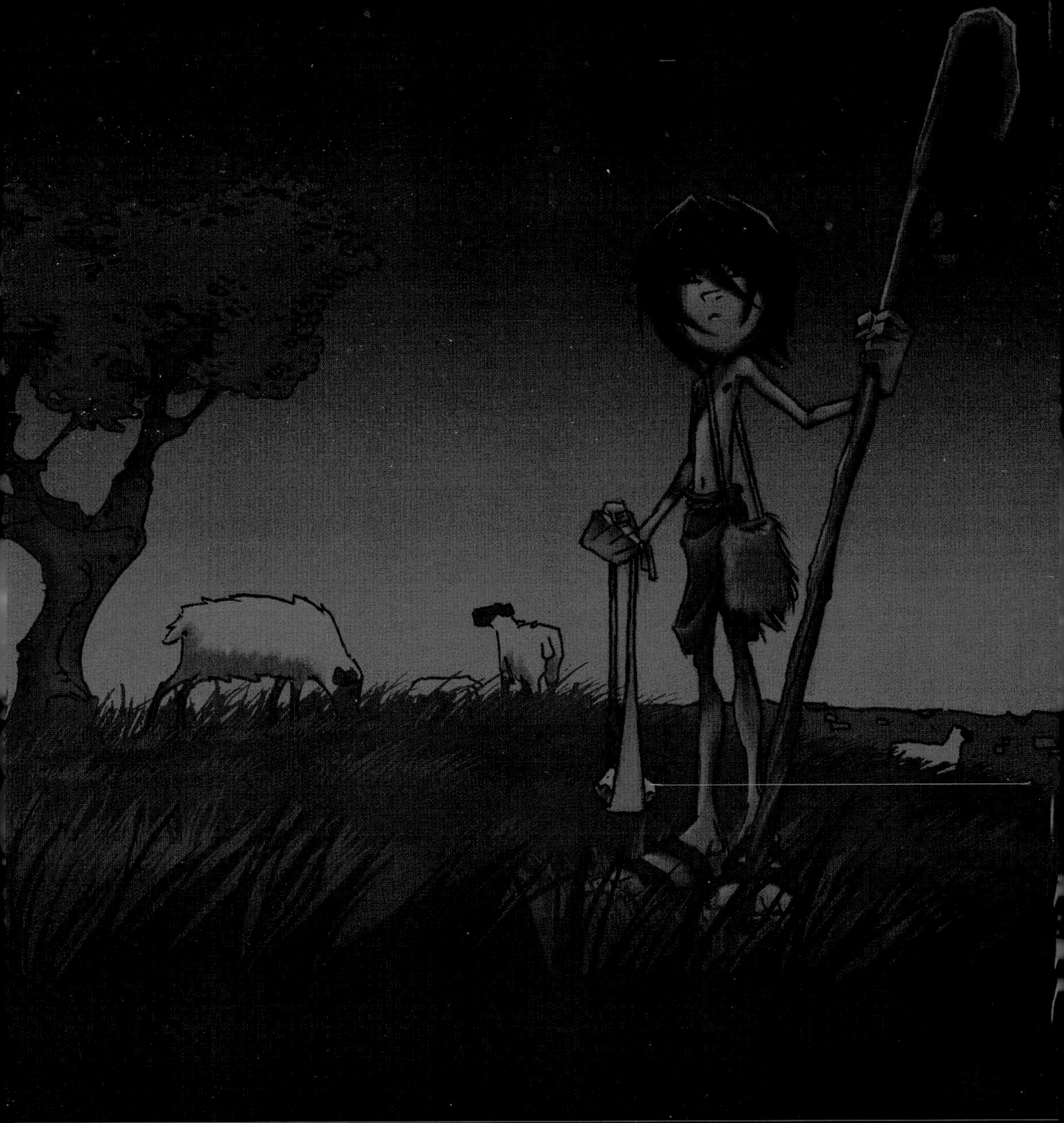

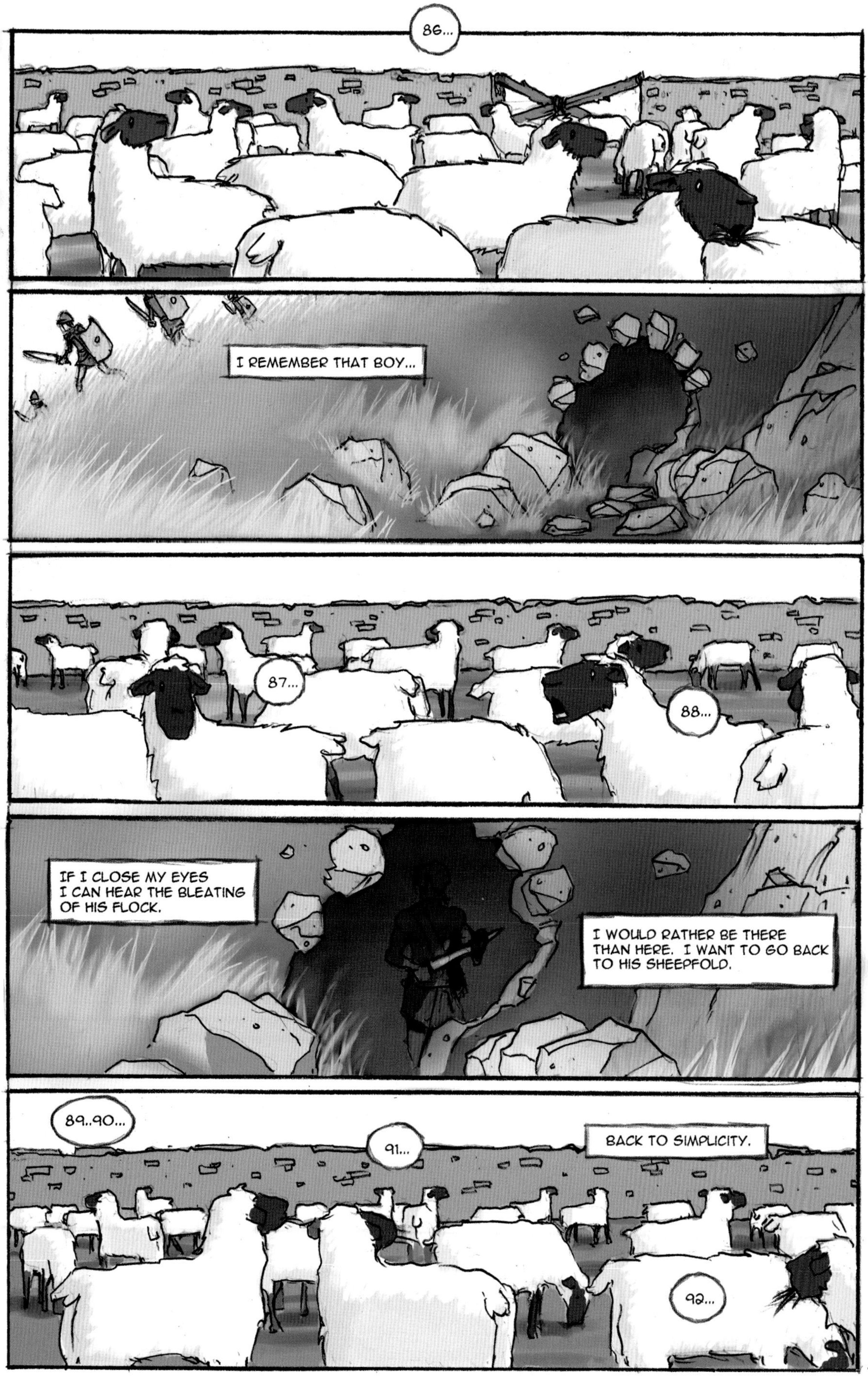
86...
I REMEMBER THAT BOY...
87...
88...
IF I CLOSE MY EYES I CAN HEAR THE BLEATING OF HIS FLOCK.
I WOULD RATHER BE THERE THAN HERE. I WANT TO GO BACK TO HIS SHEEPFOLD.
89..90...
91...
BACK TO SIMPLICITY.
92...

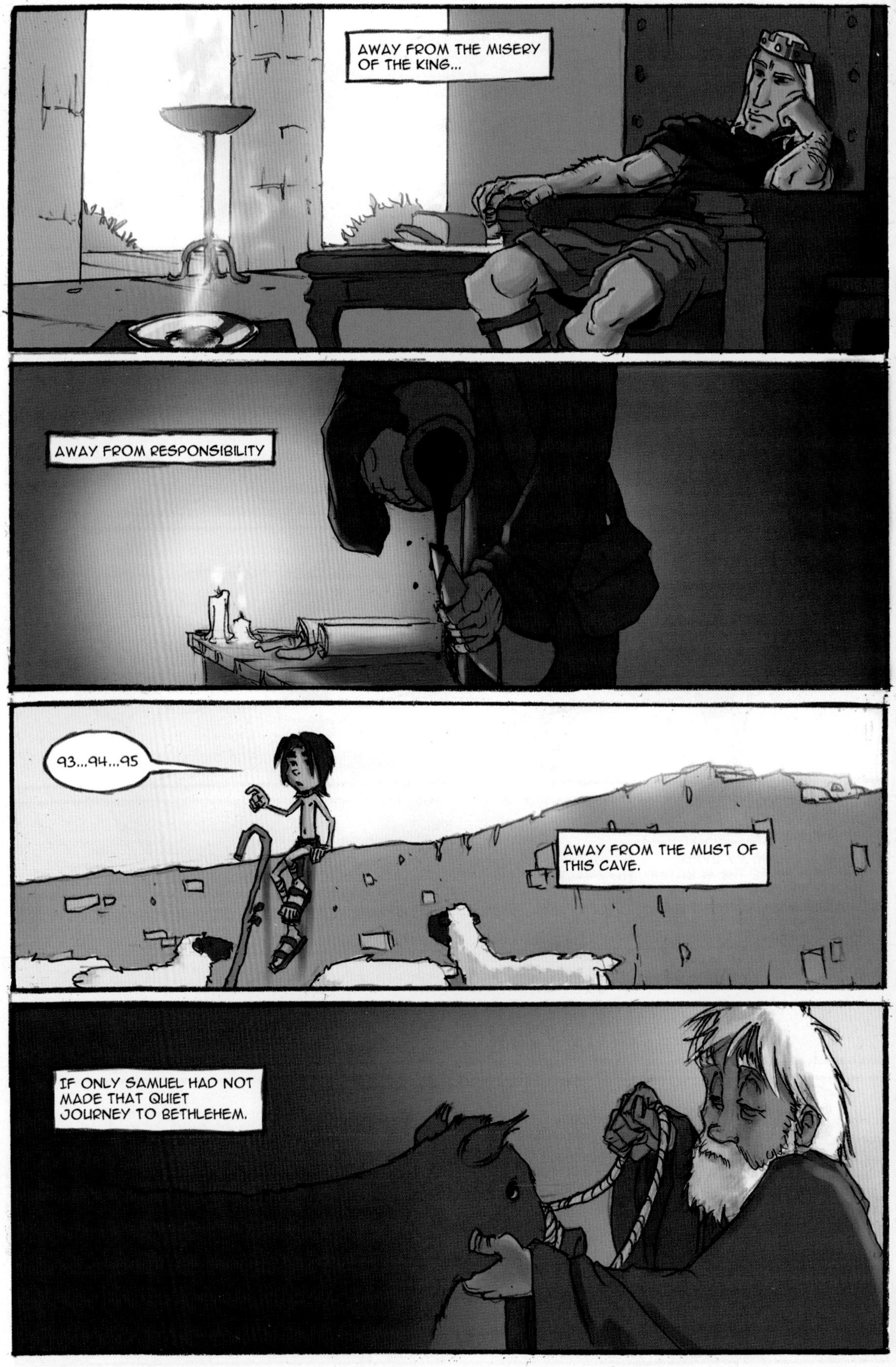
AWAY FROM THE MISERY OF THE KING...
AWAY FROM RESPONSIBILITY
93...94...95
AWAY FROM THE MUST OF THIS CAVE.
IF ONLY SAMUEL HAD NOT MADE THAT QUIET JOURNEY TO BETHLEHEM.

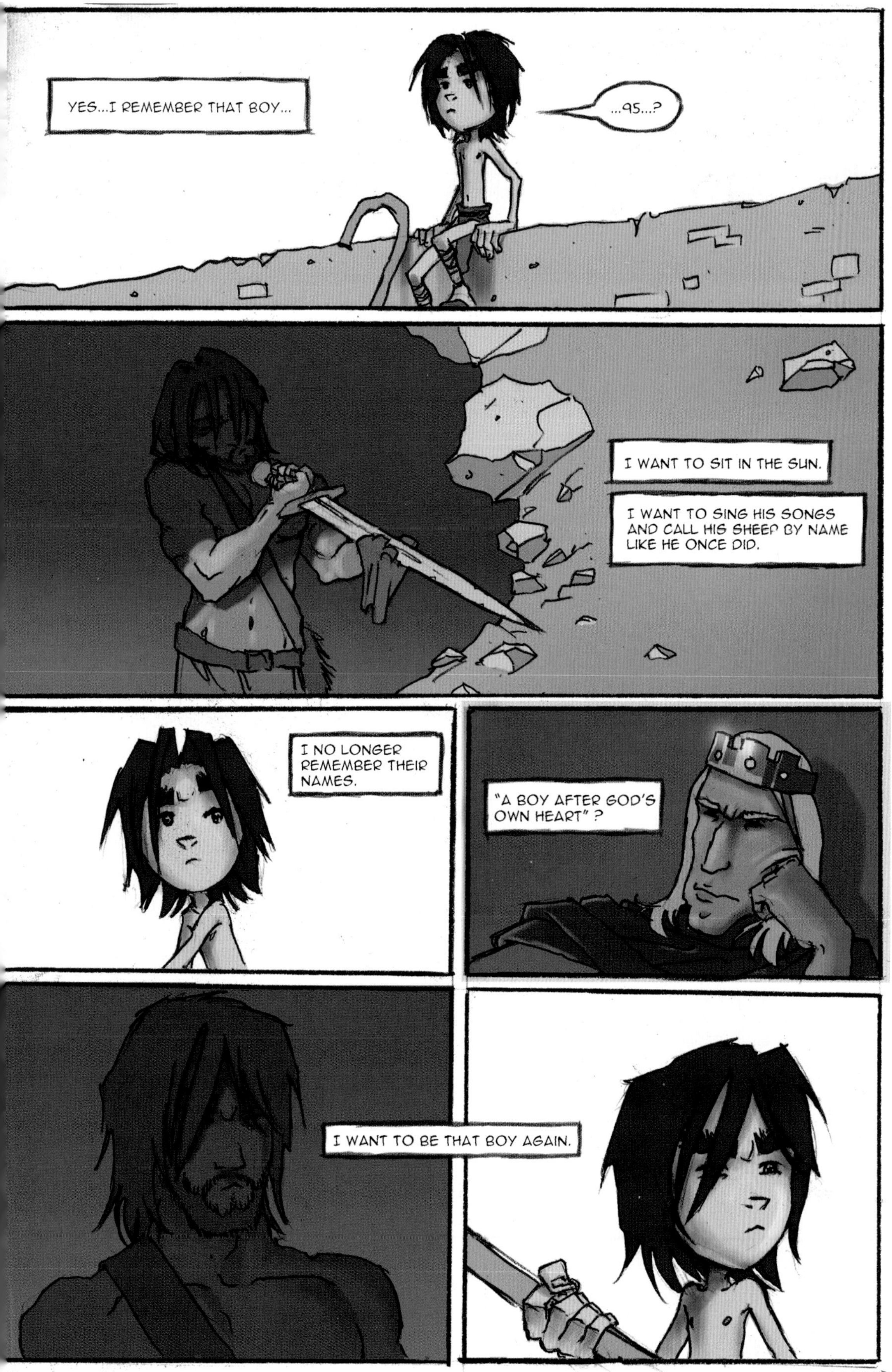
YES...I REMEMBER THAT BOY...
...95...?
I WANT TO SIT IN THE SUN.
I WANT TO SING HIS SONGS AND CALL HIS SHEEP BY NAME LIKE HE ONCE DID.
I NO LONGER REMEMBER THEIR NAMES.
"A BOY AFTER GOD'S OWN HEART" ?
I WANT TO BE THAT BOY AGAIN.

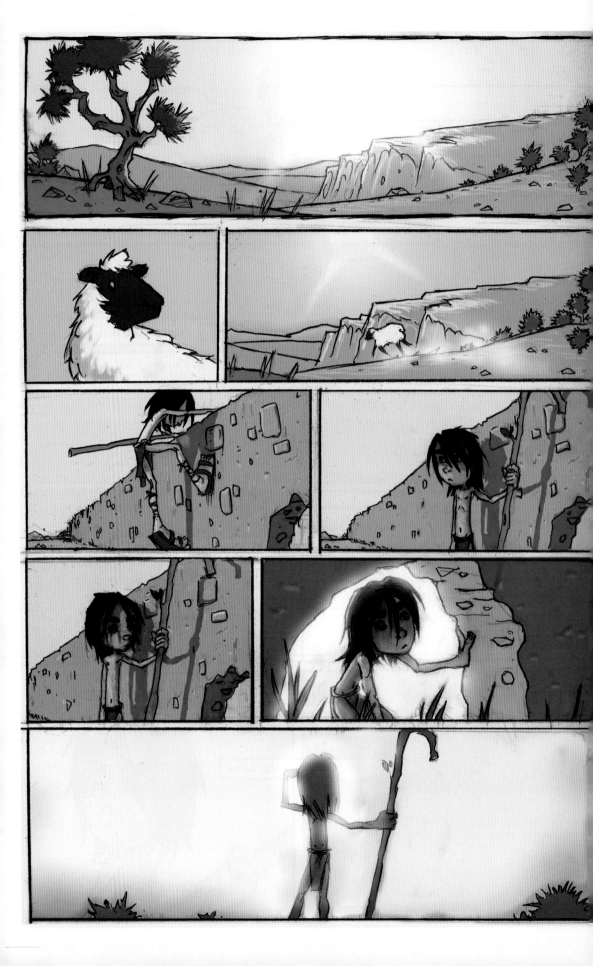

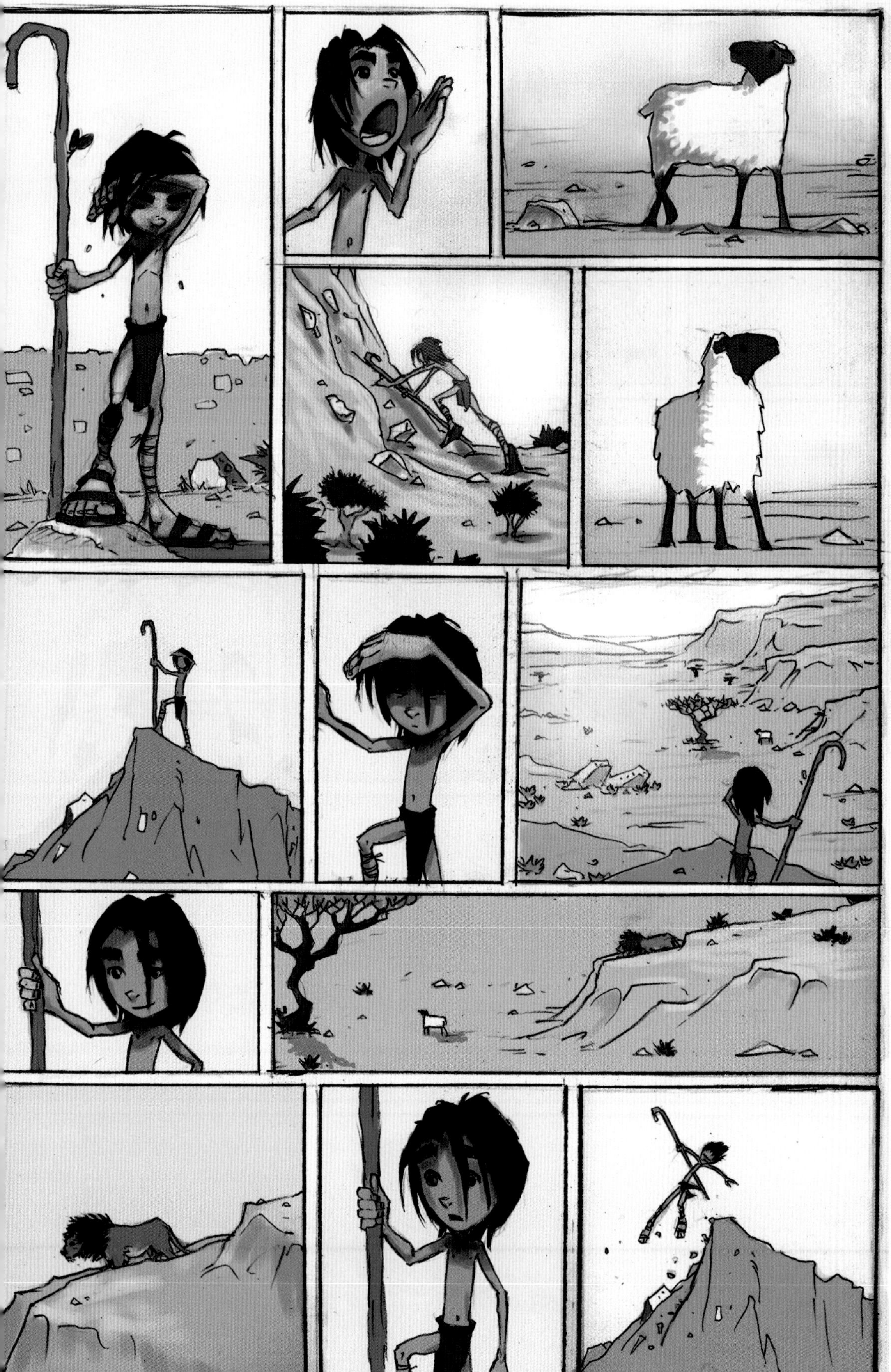

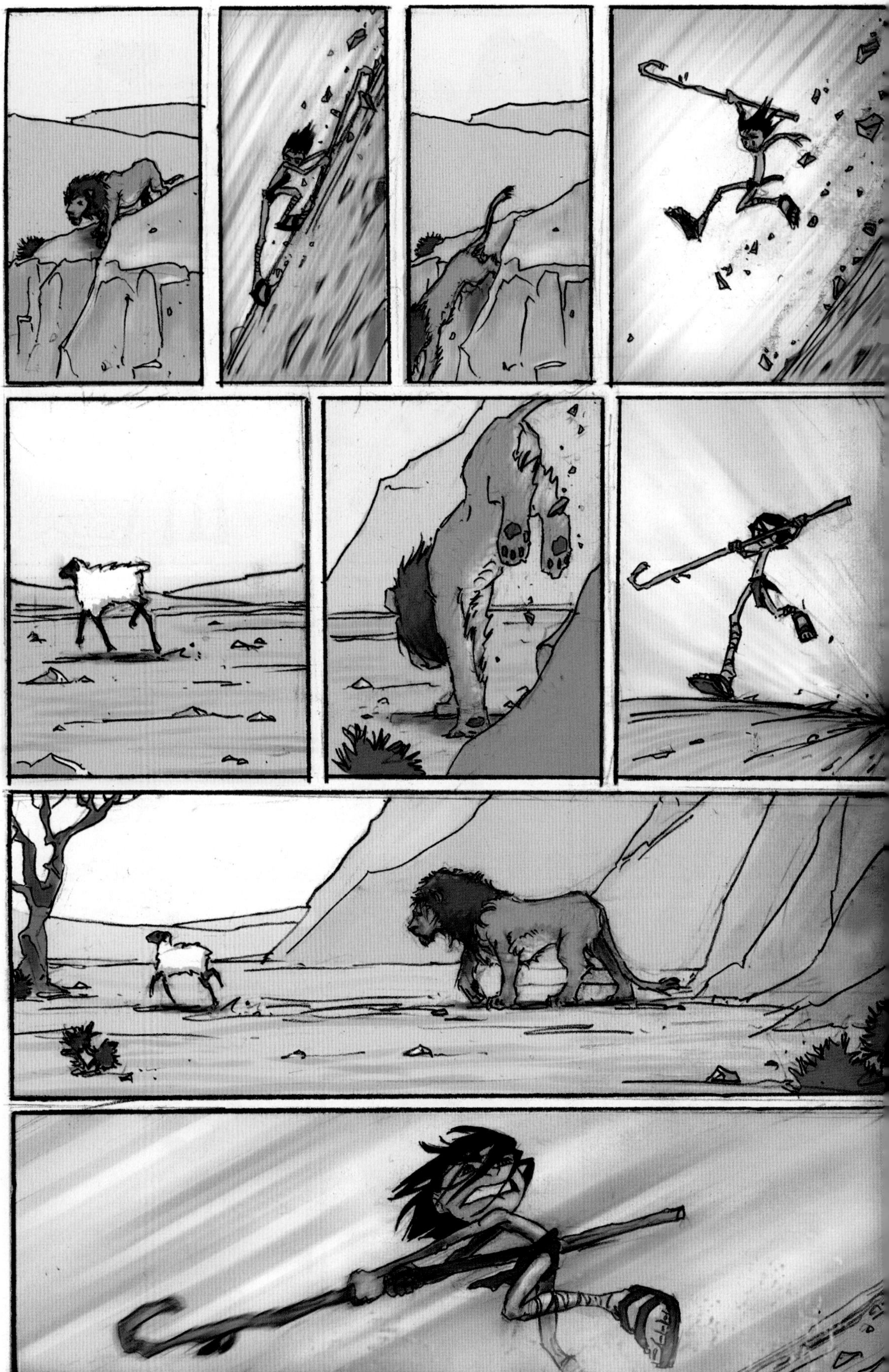

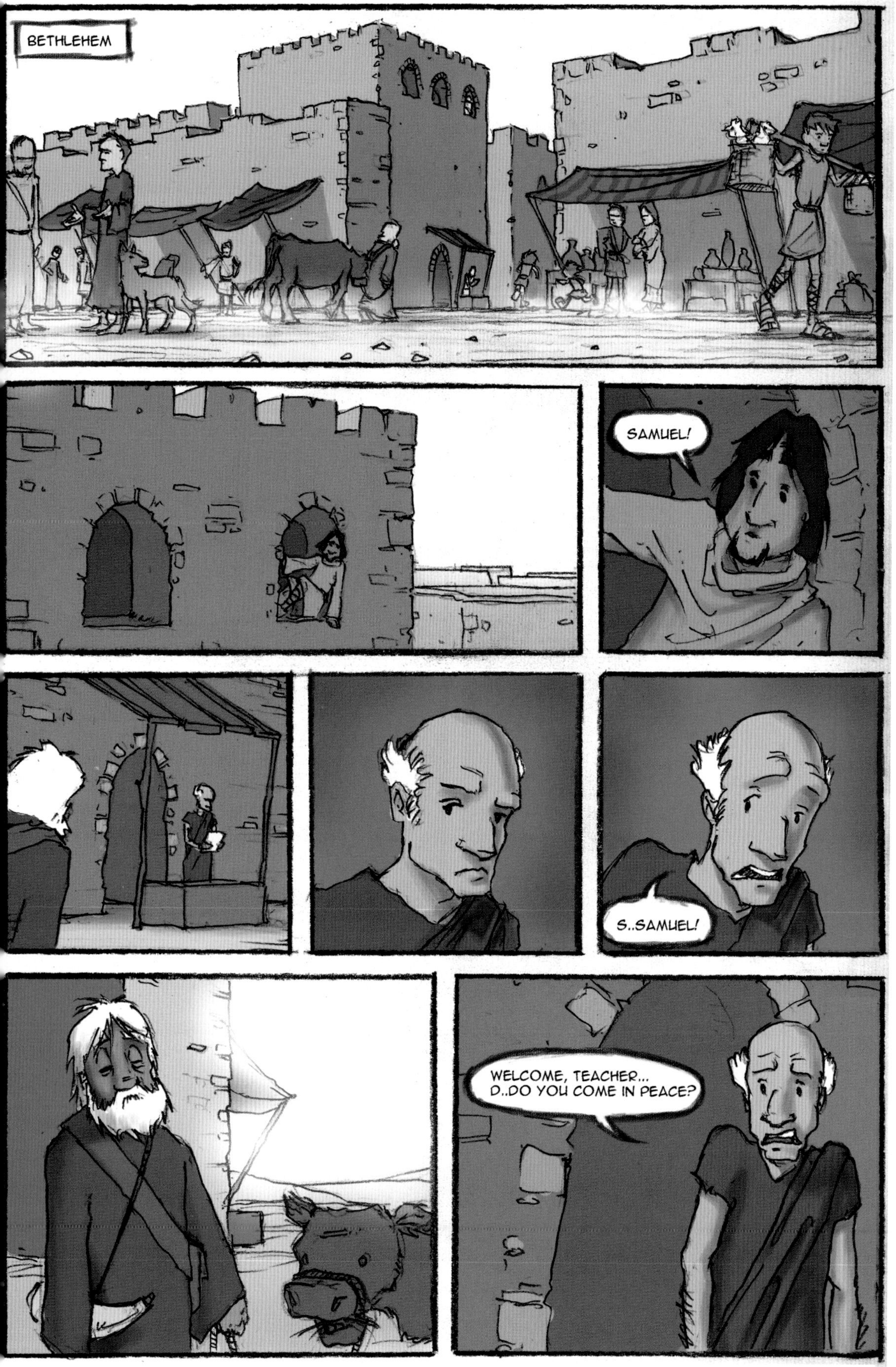
BETHLEHEM
SAMUEL!
S..SAMUEL!
WELCOME, TEACHER...
D..DO YOU COME IN PEACE?

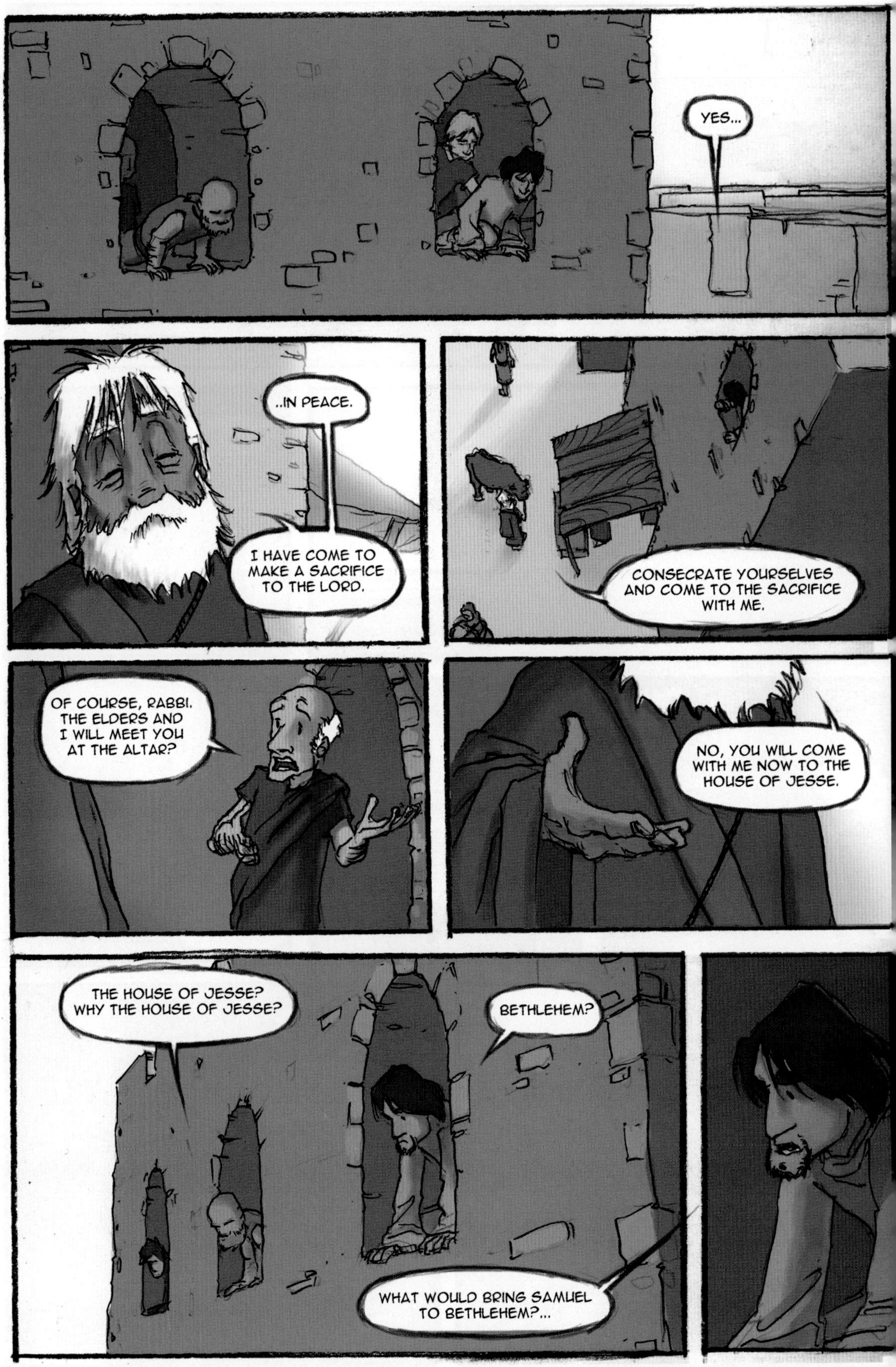
YES...
..IN PEACE.
I HAVE COME TO MAKE A SACRIFICE TO THE LORD.
CONSECRATE YOURSELVES AND COME TO THE SACRIFICE WITH ME.
OF COURSE, RABBI. THE ELDERS AND I WILL MEET YOU AT THE ALTAR?
NO, YOU WILL COME WITH ME NOW TO THE HOUSE OF JESSE.
THE HOUSE OF JESSE? WHY THE HOUSE OF JESSE?
BETHLEHEM?
WHAT WOULD BRING SAMUEL TO BETHLEHEM?...

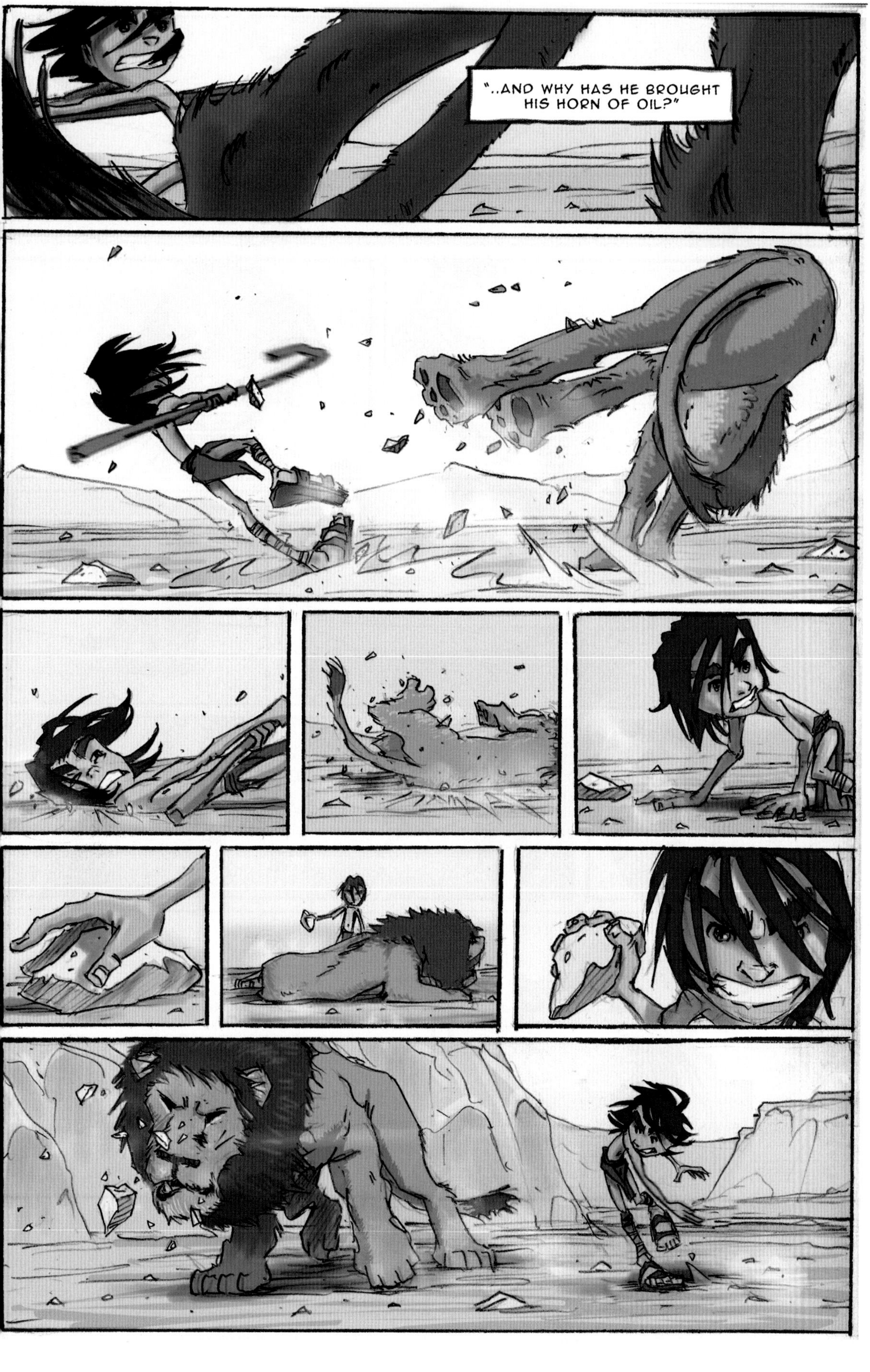
"..AND WHY HAS HE BROUGHT HIS HORN OF OIL?"

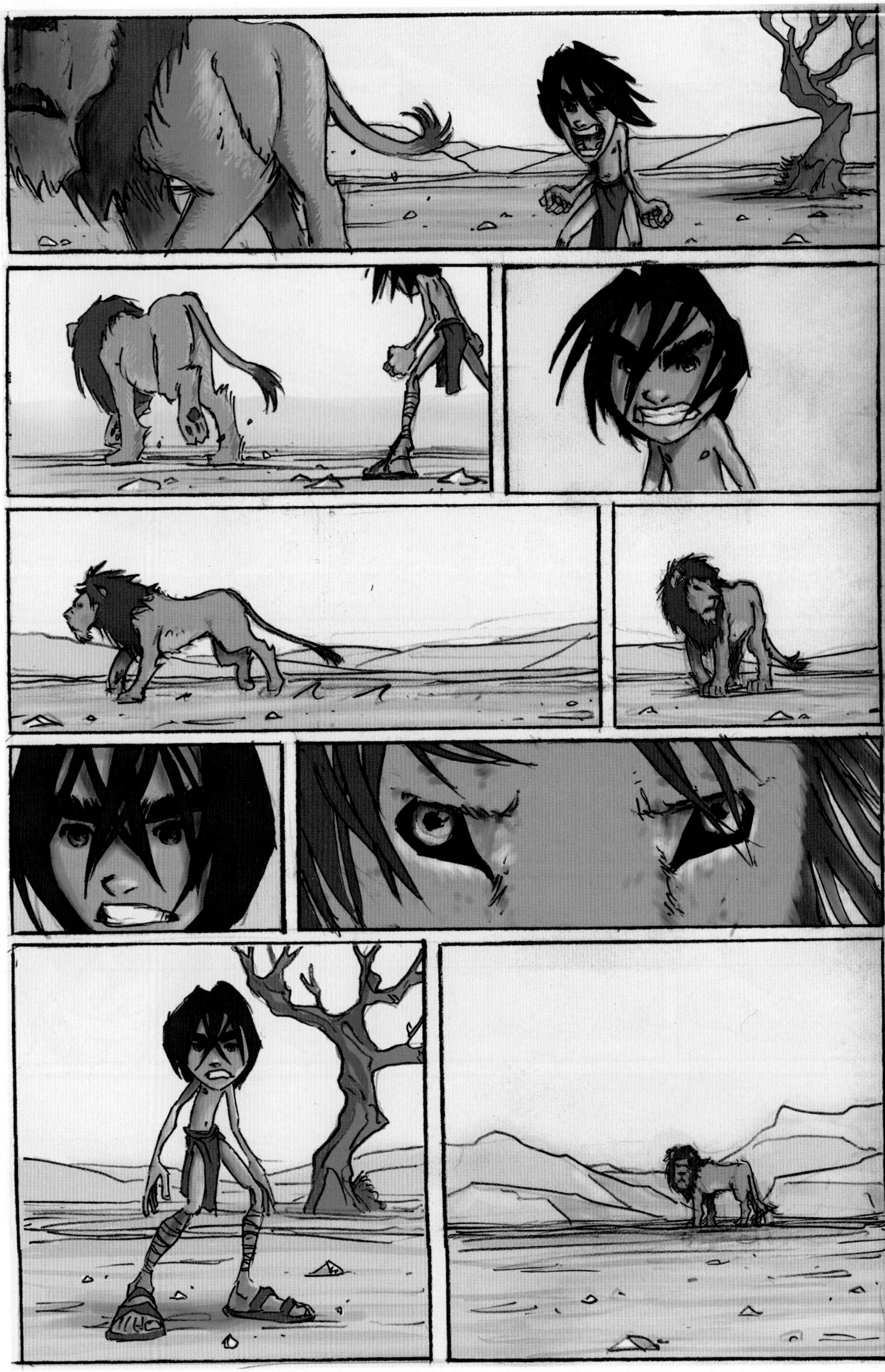

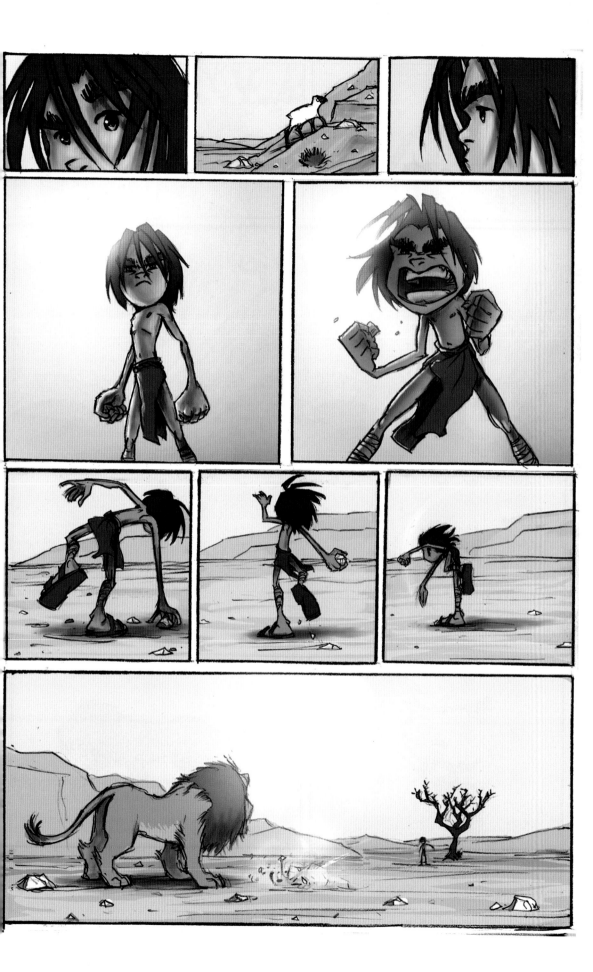

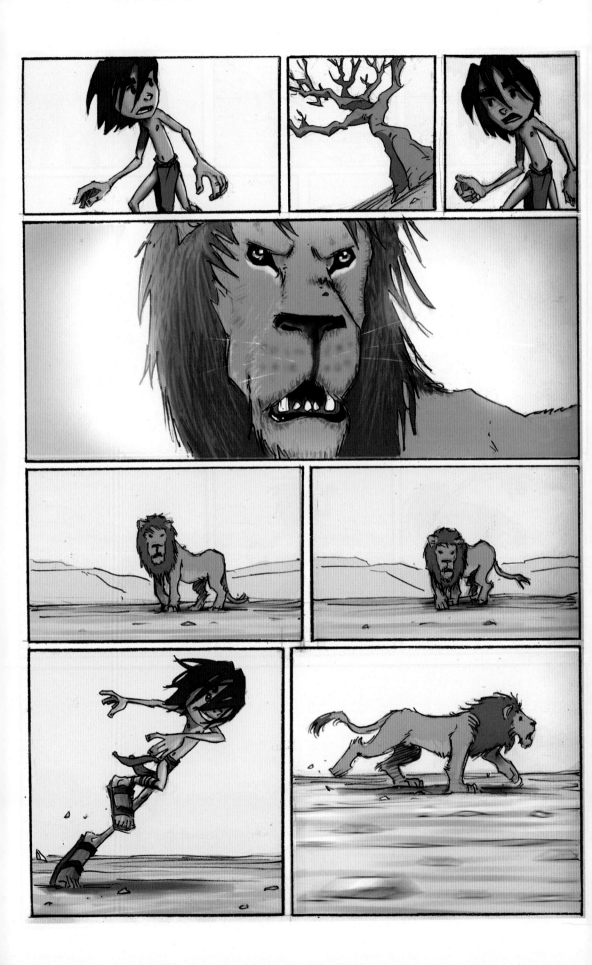

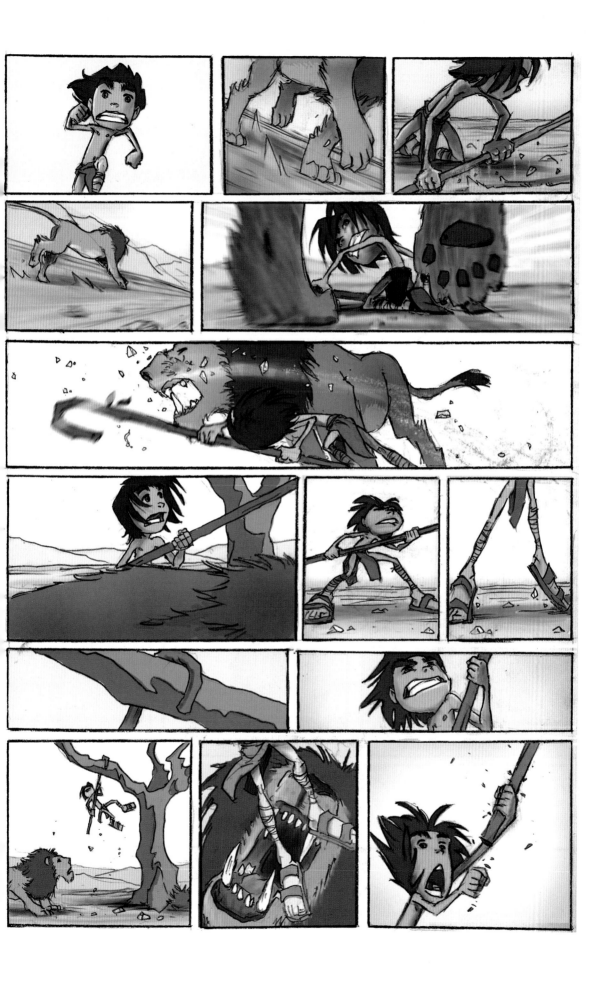

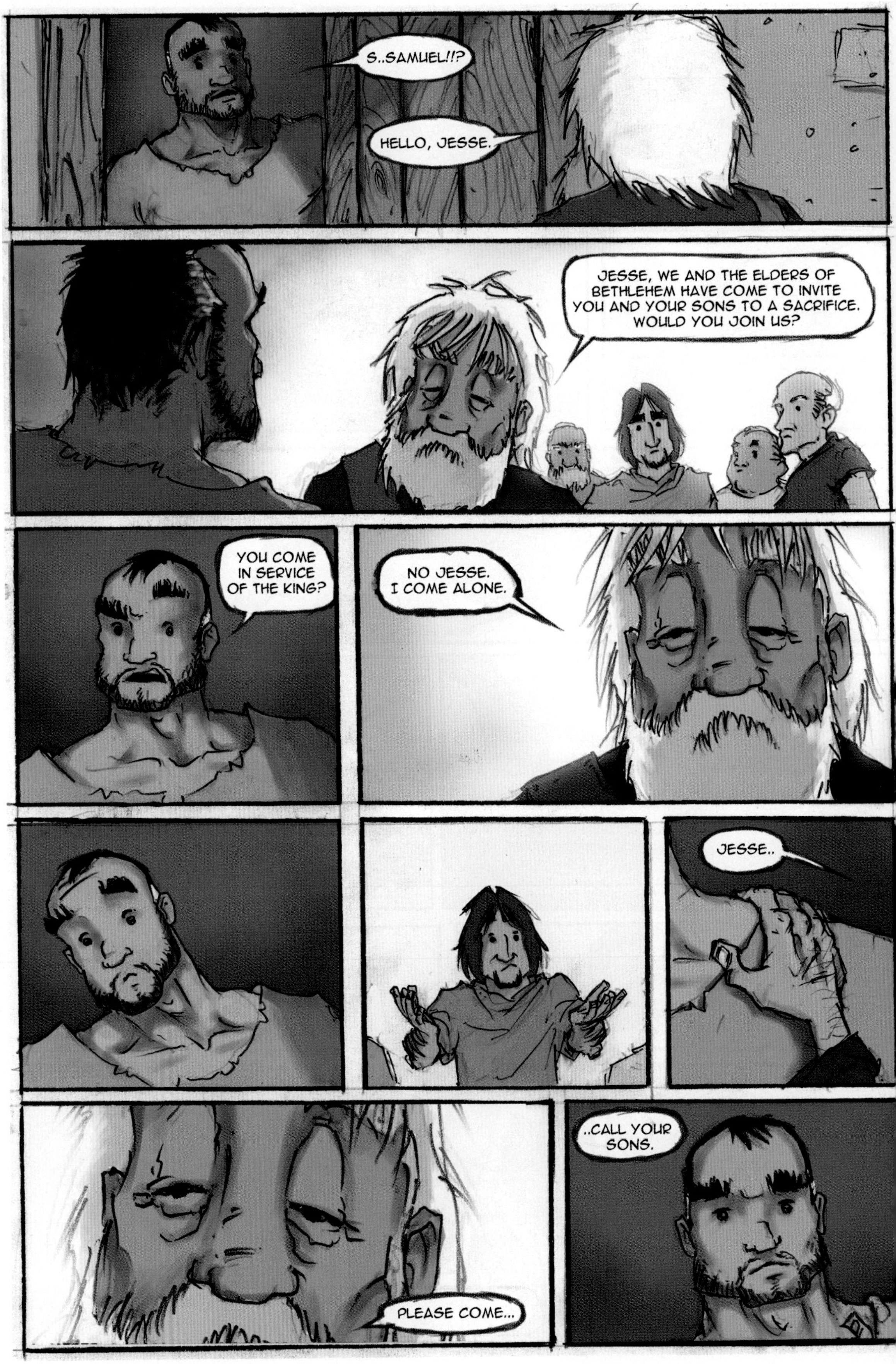
S..SAMUEL!!?
HELLO, JESSE.
JESSE, WE AND THE ELDERS OF BETHLEHEM HAVE COME TO INVITE YOU AND YOUR SONS TO A SACRIFICE. WOULD YOU JOIN US?
YOU COME IN SERVICE OF THE KING?
NO JESSE. I COME ALONE.
JESSE..
PLEASE COME...
..CALL YOUR SONS.

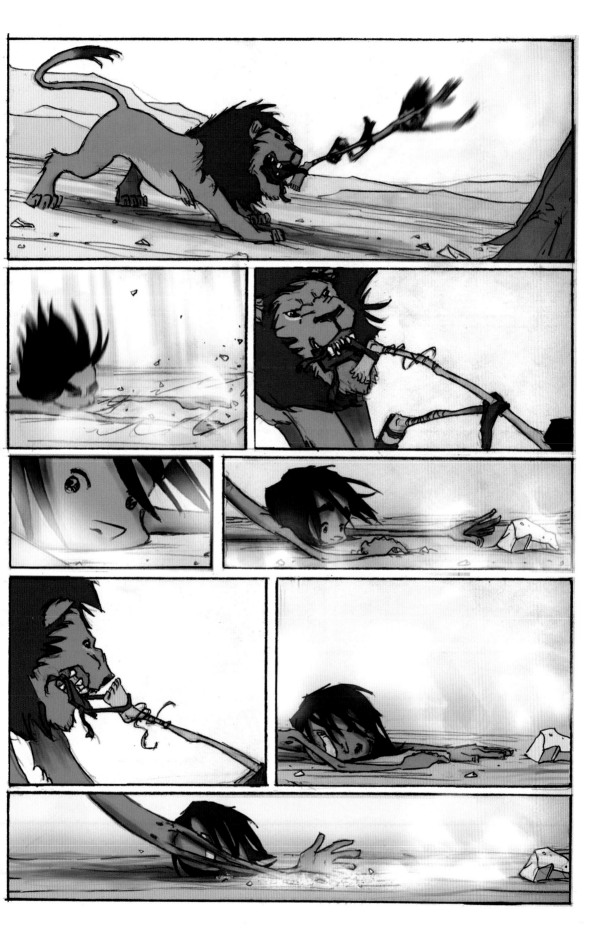

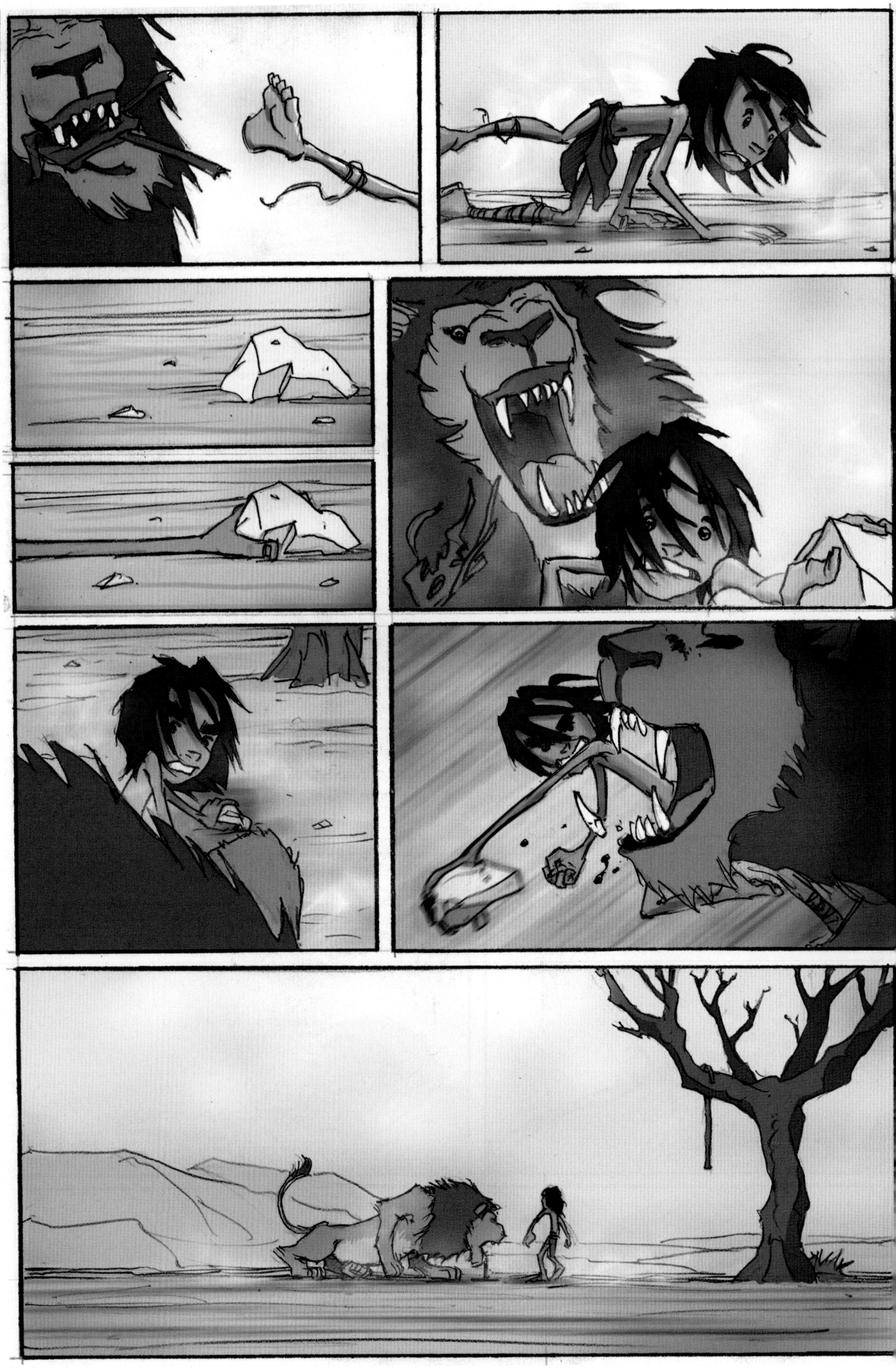

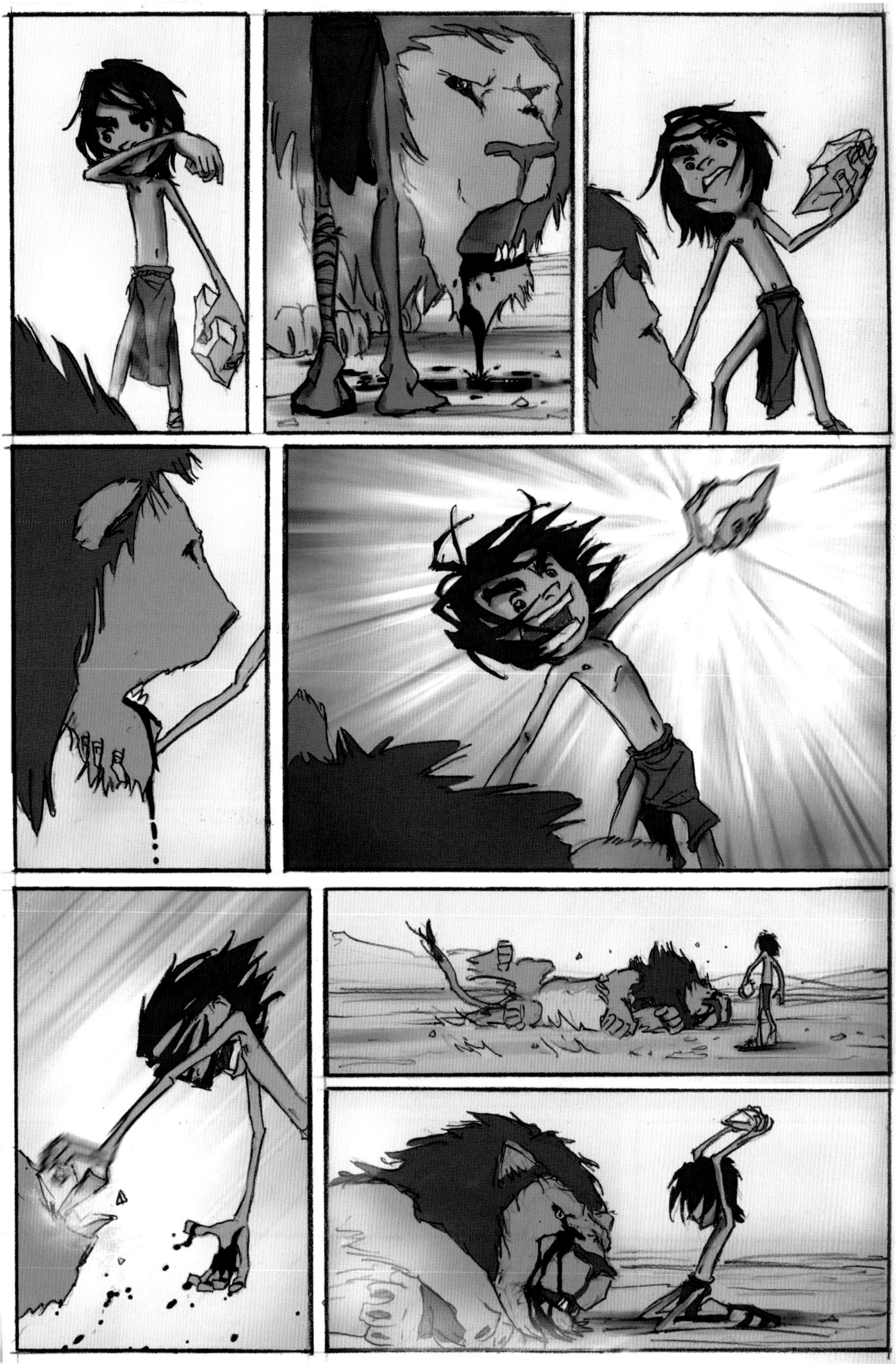

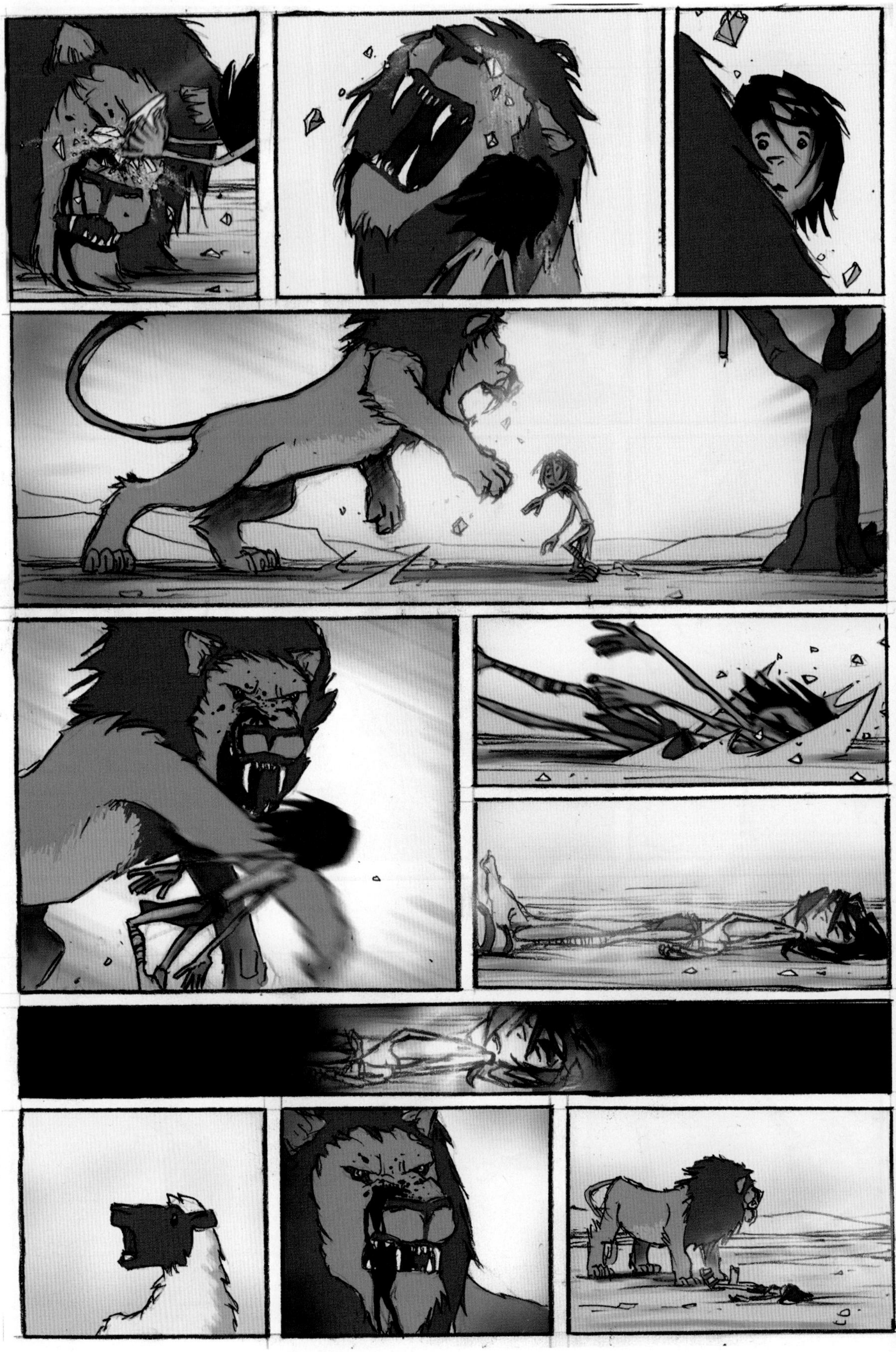

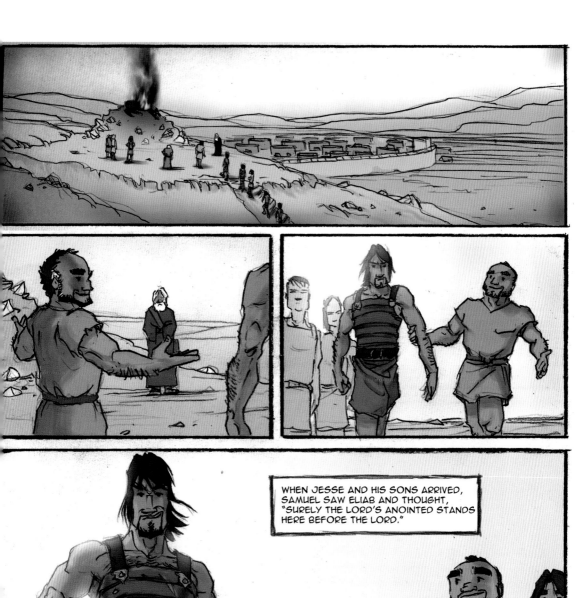

WHEN JESSE AND HIS SONS ARRIVED, SAMUEL SAW ELIAB AND THOUGHT, "SURELY THE LORD'S ANOINTED STANDS HERE BEFORE THE LORD."

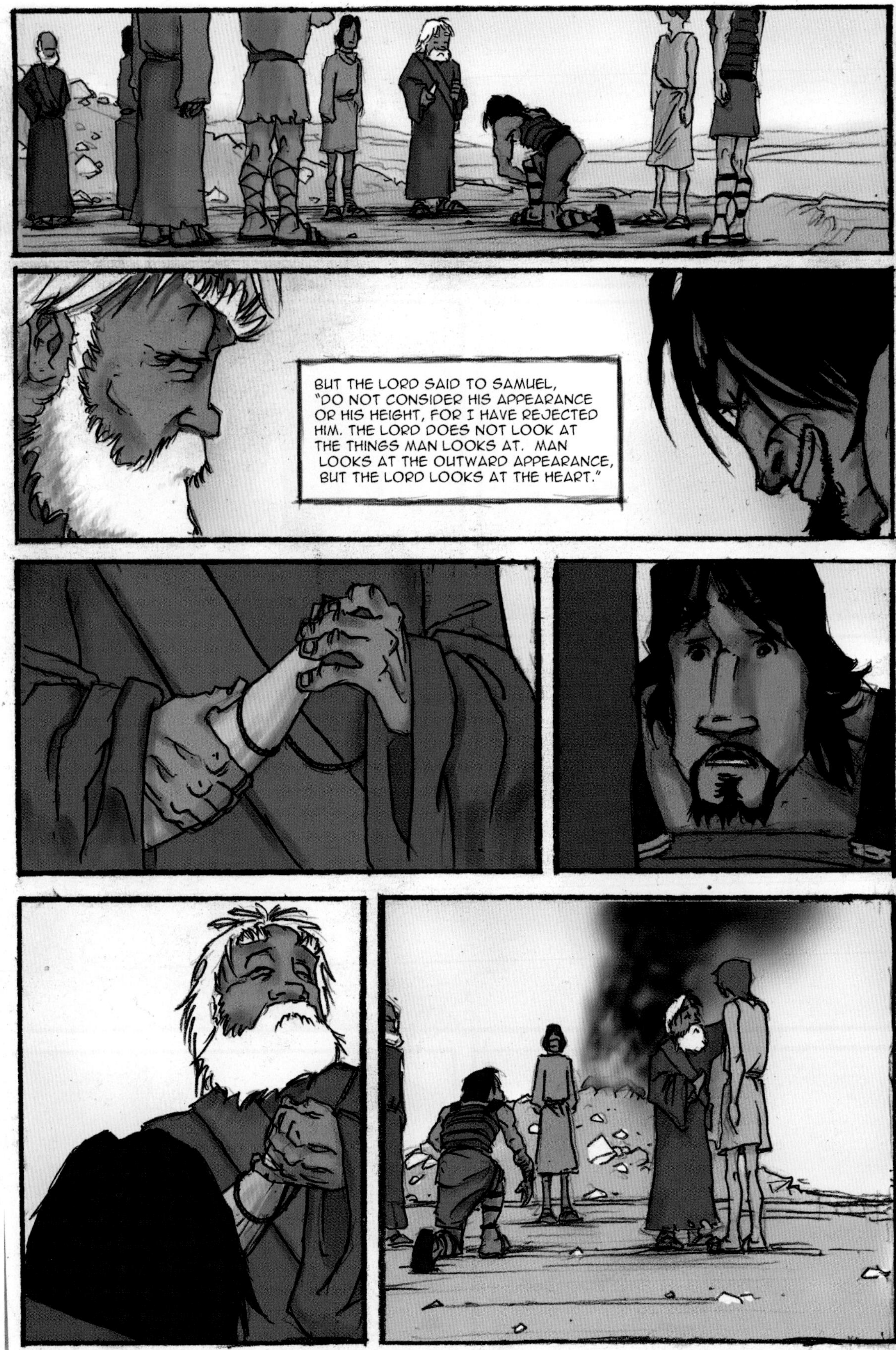
BUT THE LORD SAID TO SAMUEL, "DO NOT CONSIDER HIS APPEARANCE OR HIS HEIGHT, FOR I HAVE REJECTED HIM. THE LORD DOES NOT LOOK AT THE THINGS MAN LOOKS AT. MAN LOOKS AT THE OUTWARD APPEARANCE, BUT THE LORD LOOKS AT THE HEART."

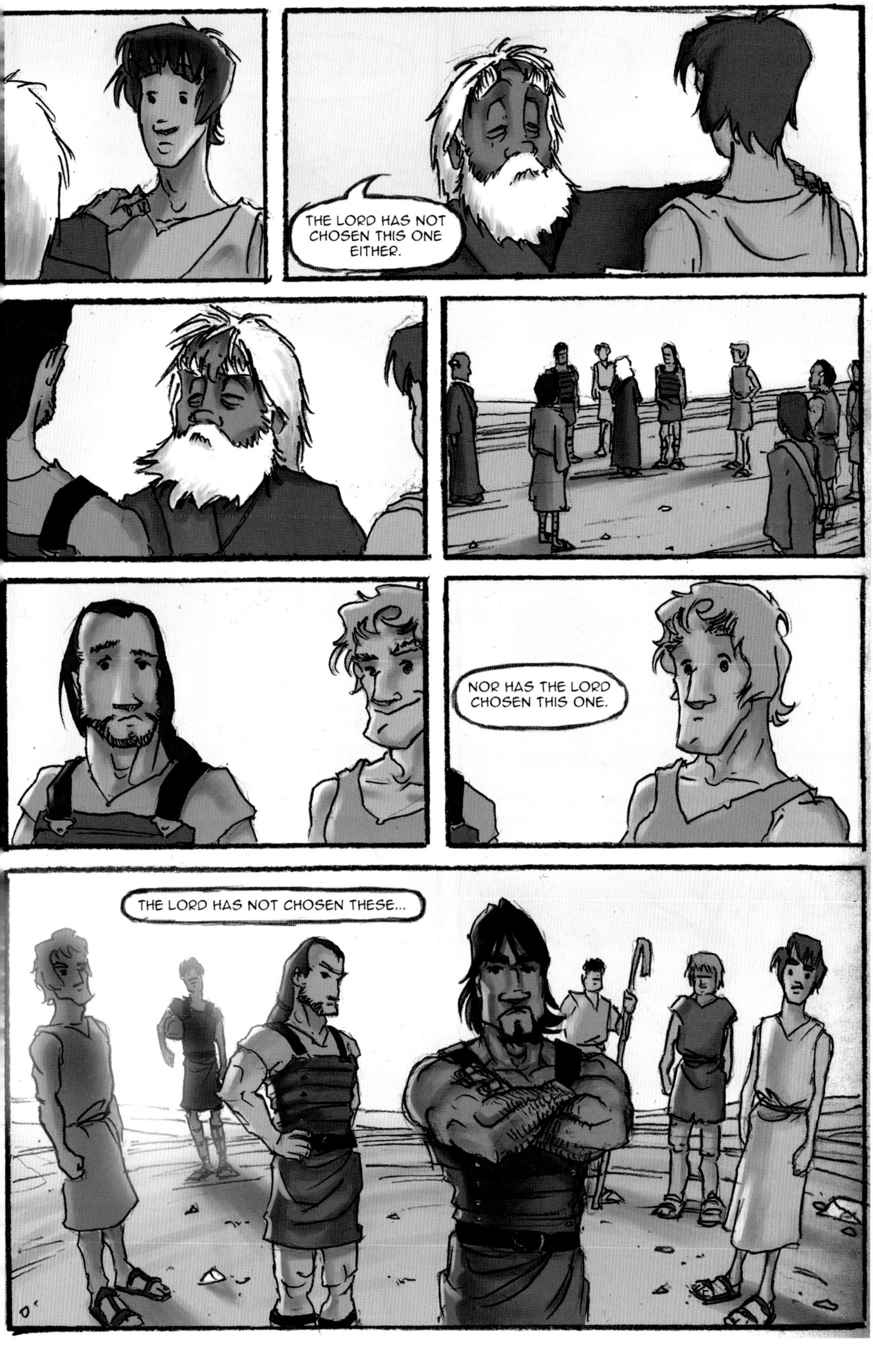
THE LORD HAS NOT CHOSEN THIS ONE EITHER.
NOR HAS THE LORD CHOSEN THIS ONE.
THE LORD HAS NOT CHOSEN THESE...

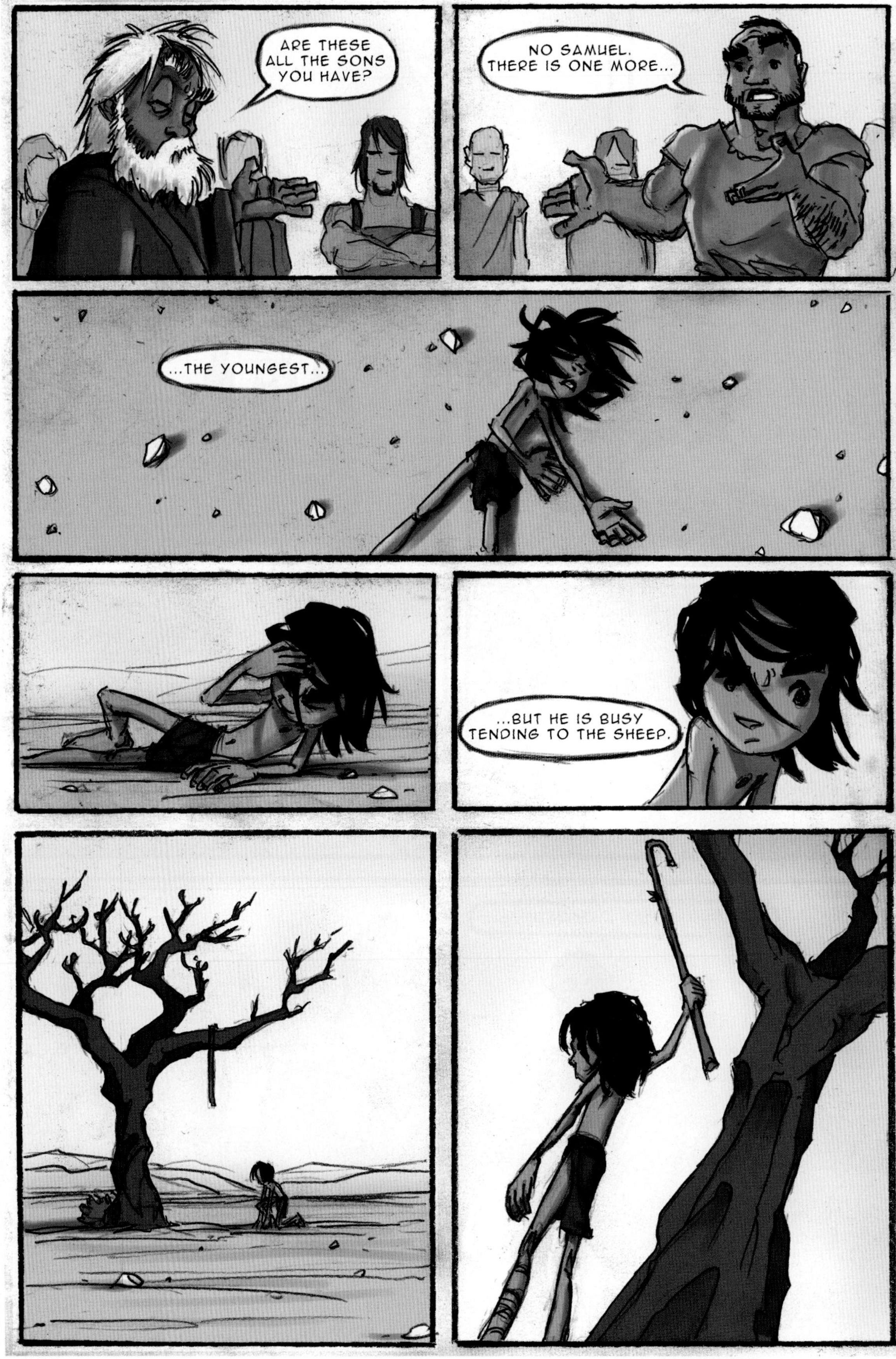
ARE THESE ALL THE SONS YOU HAVE?
NO SAMUEL. THERE IS ONE MORE...
...THE YOUNGEST...
...BUT HE IS BUSY TENDING TO THE SHEEP.

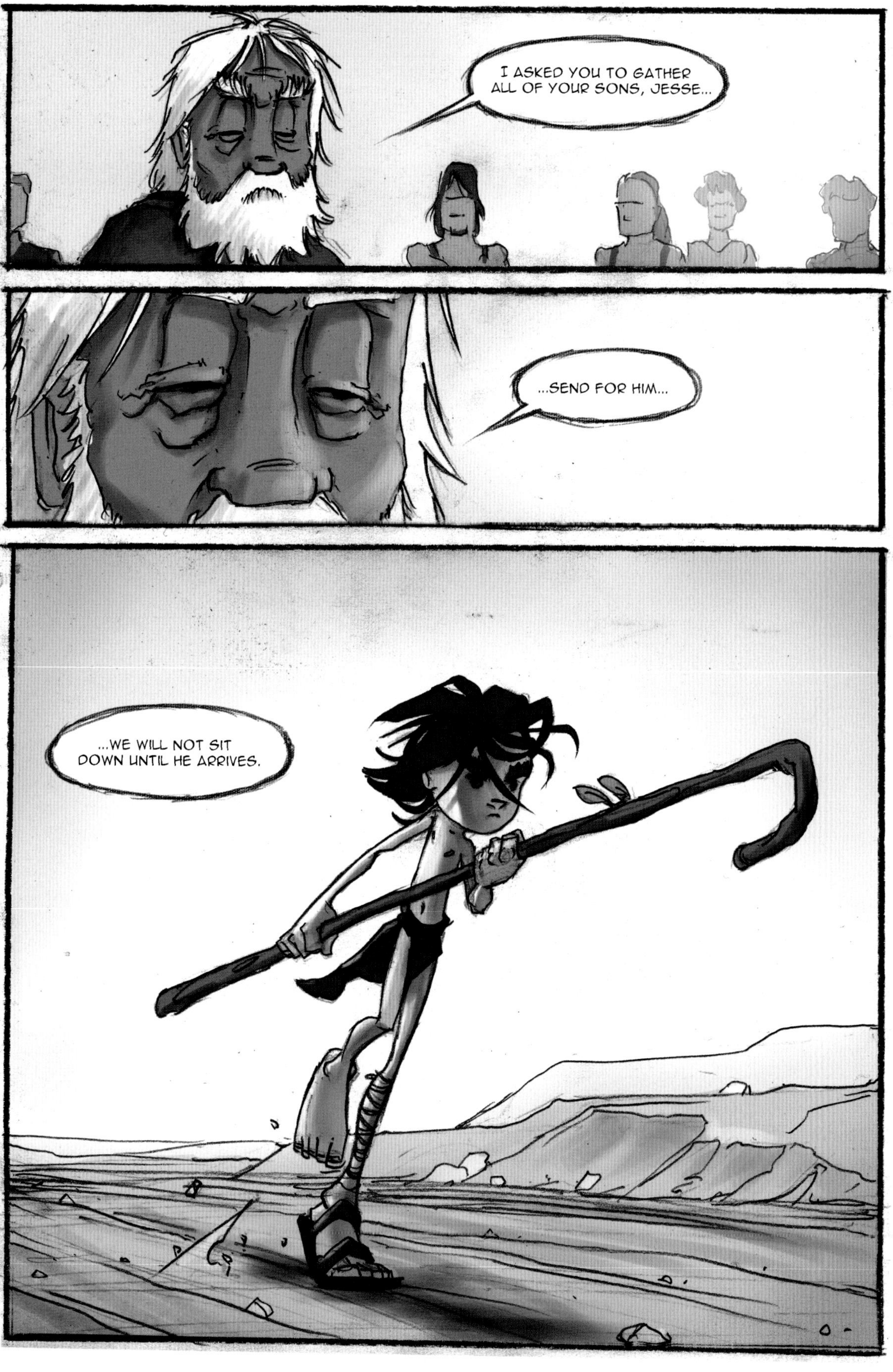
I ASKED YOU TO GATHER ALL OF YOUR SONS, JESSE...
...SEND FOR HIM...
...WE WILL NOT SIT DOWN UNTIL HE ARRIVES.

CHAPTER 2

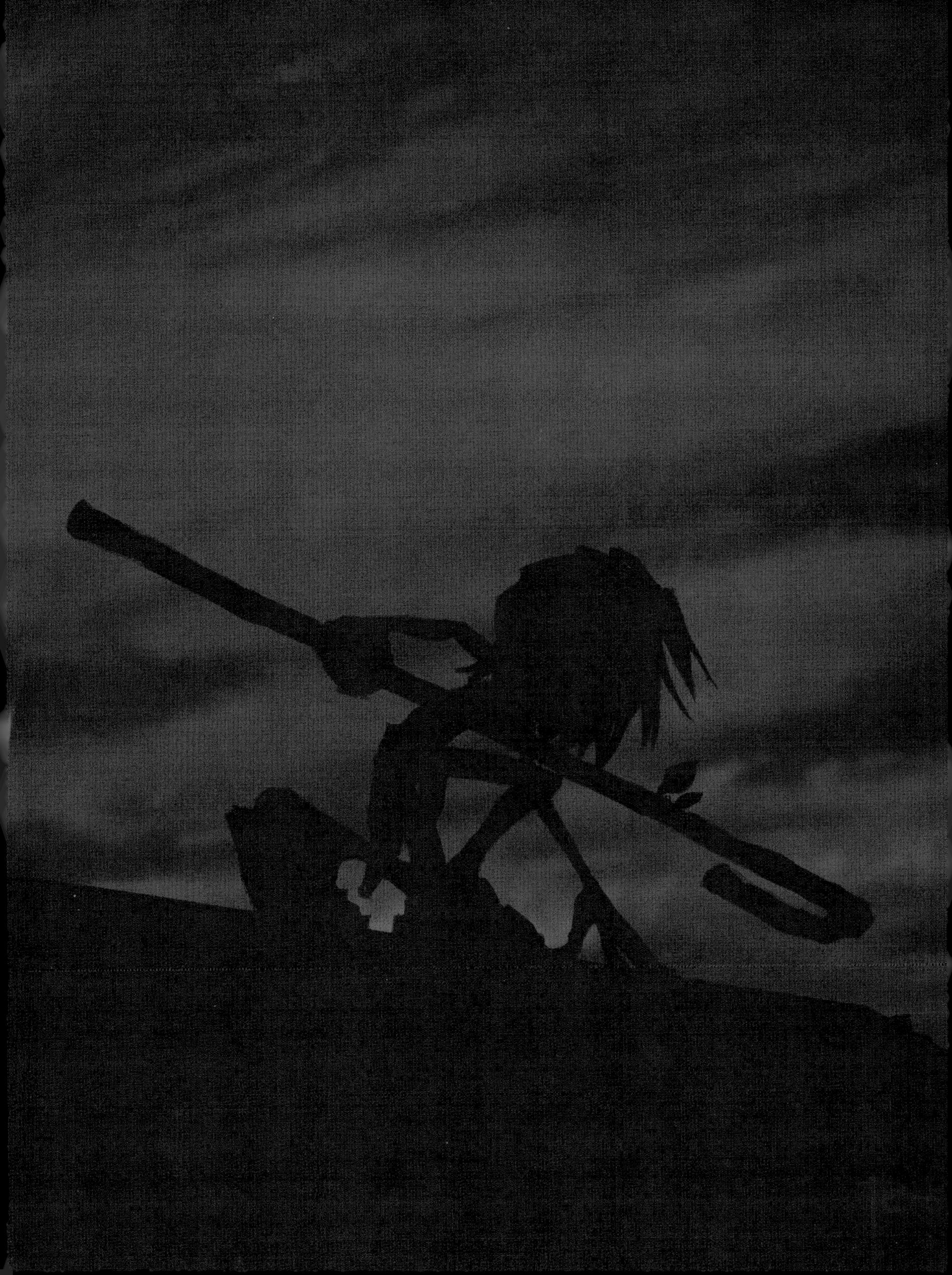

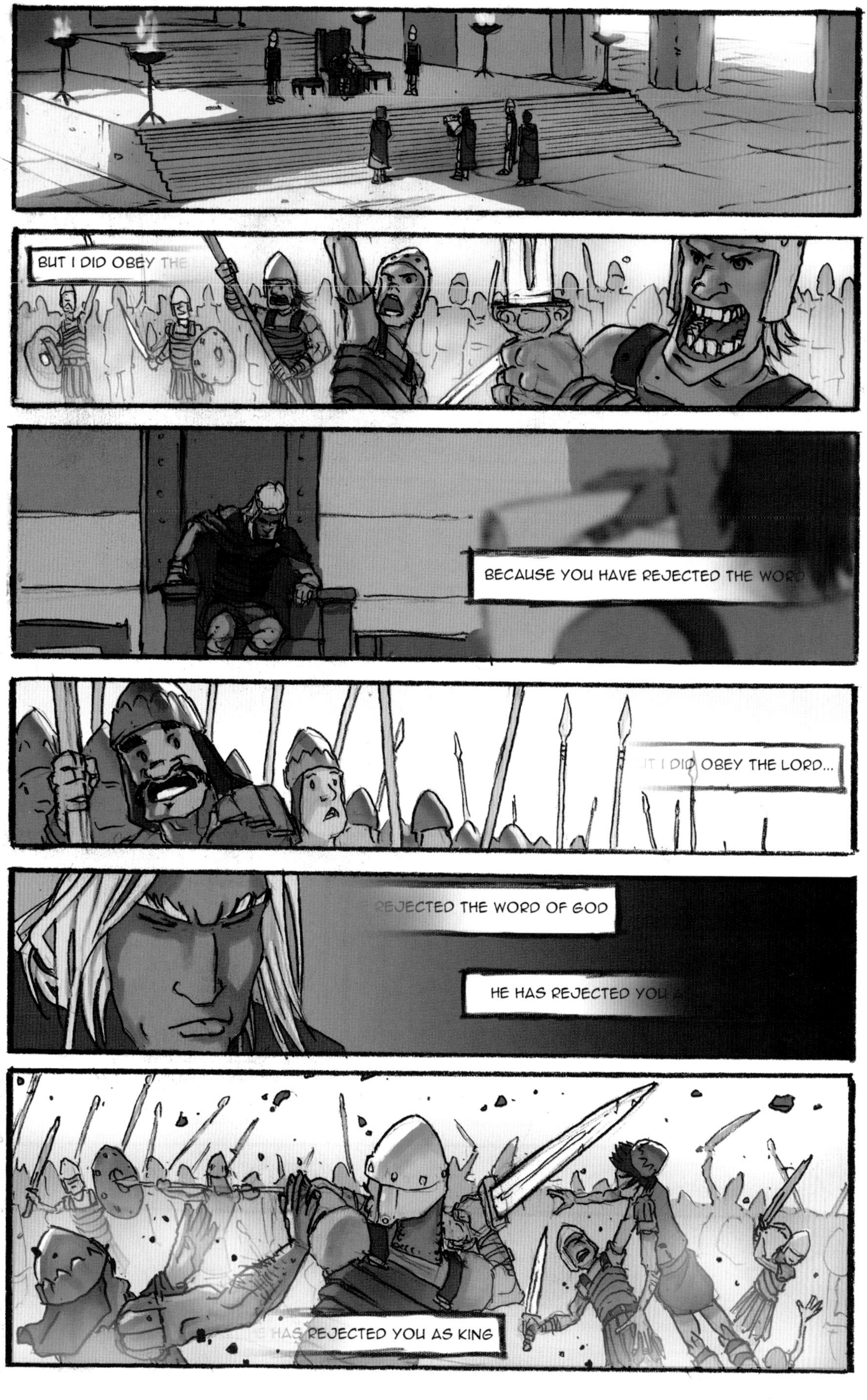
BUT I DID OBEY THE
BECAUSE YOU HAVE REJECTED THE WOR
UT I DID OBEY THE LORD...
EJECTED THE WORD OF GOD
HE HAS REJECTED YOU
HAS REJECTED YOU AS KING

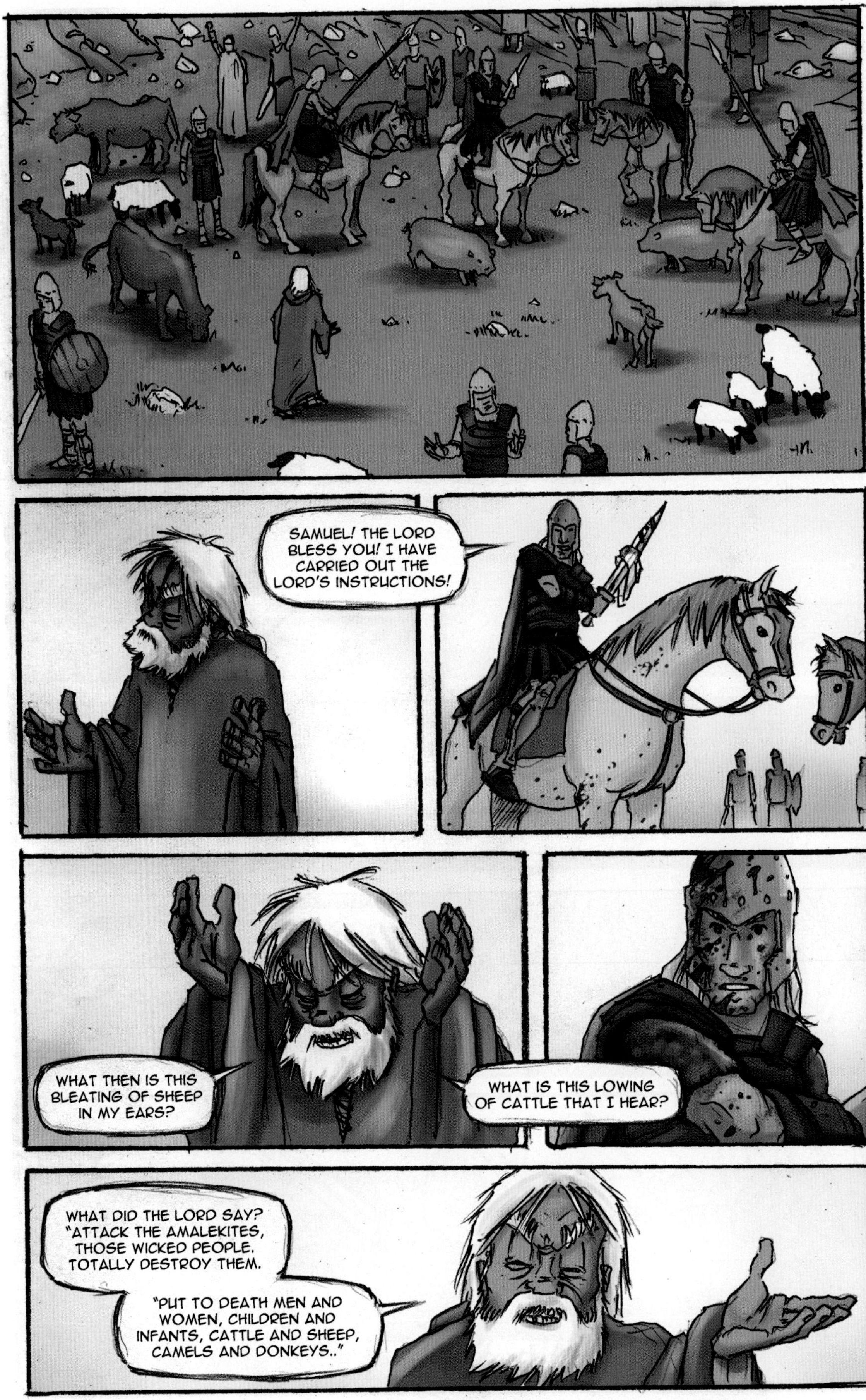
SAMUEL! THE LORD BLESS YOU! I HAVE CARRIED OUT THE LORD'S INSTRUCTIONS!
WHAT THEN IS THIS BLEATING OF SHEEP IN MY EARS?
WHAT IS THIS LOWING OF CATTLE THAT I HEAR?
WHAT DID THE LORD SAY? "ATTACK THE AMALEKITES, THOSE WICKED PEOPLE. TOTALLY DESTROY THEM.
"PUT TO DEATH MEN AND WOMEN, CHILDREN AND INFANTS, CATTLE AND SHEEP, CAMELS AND DONKEYS.."

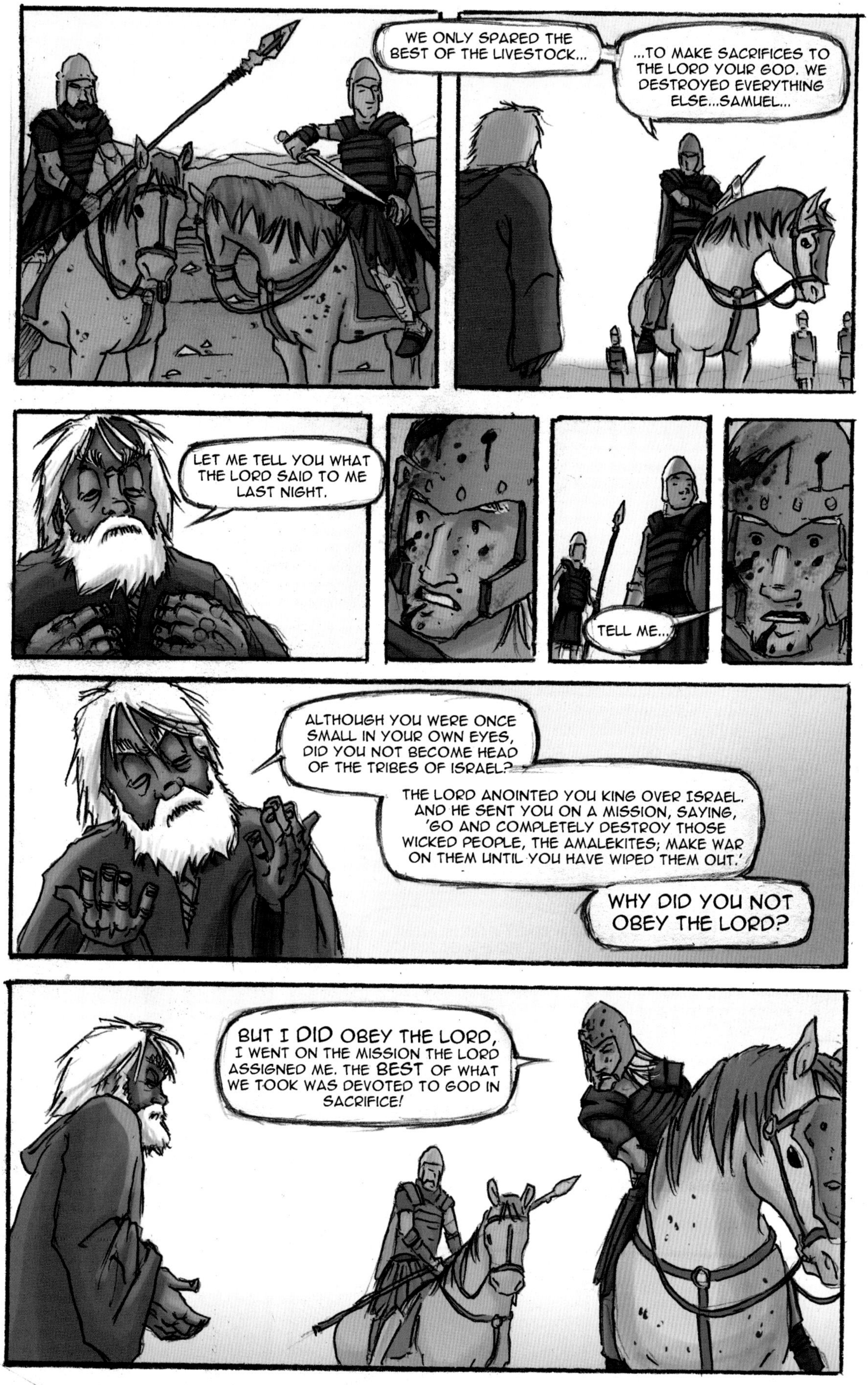
WE ONLY SPARED THE BEST OF THE LIVESTOCK...
...TO MAKE SACRIFICES TO THE LORD YOUR GOD. WE DESTROYED EVERYTHING ELSE...SAMUEL...
LET ME TELL YOU WHAT THE LORD SAID TO ME LAST NIGHT.
TELL ME...
ALTHOUGH YOU WERE ONCE SMALL IN YOUR OWN EYES, DID YOU NOT BECOME HEAD OF THE TRIBES OF ISRAEL?
THE LORD ANOINTED YOU KING OVER ISRAEL. AND HE SENT YOU ON A MISSION, SAYING, 'GO AND COMPLETELY DESTROY THOSE WICKED PEOPLE, THE AMALEKITES; MAKE WAR ON THEM UNTIL YOU HAVE WIPED THEM OUT.'
WHY DID YOU NOT OBEY THE LORD?
BUT I DID OBEY THE LORD, I WENT ON THE MISSION THE LORD ASSIGNED ME. THE BEST OF WHAT WE TOOK WAS DEVOTED TO GOD IN SACRIFICE!

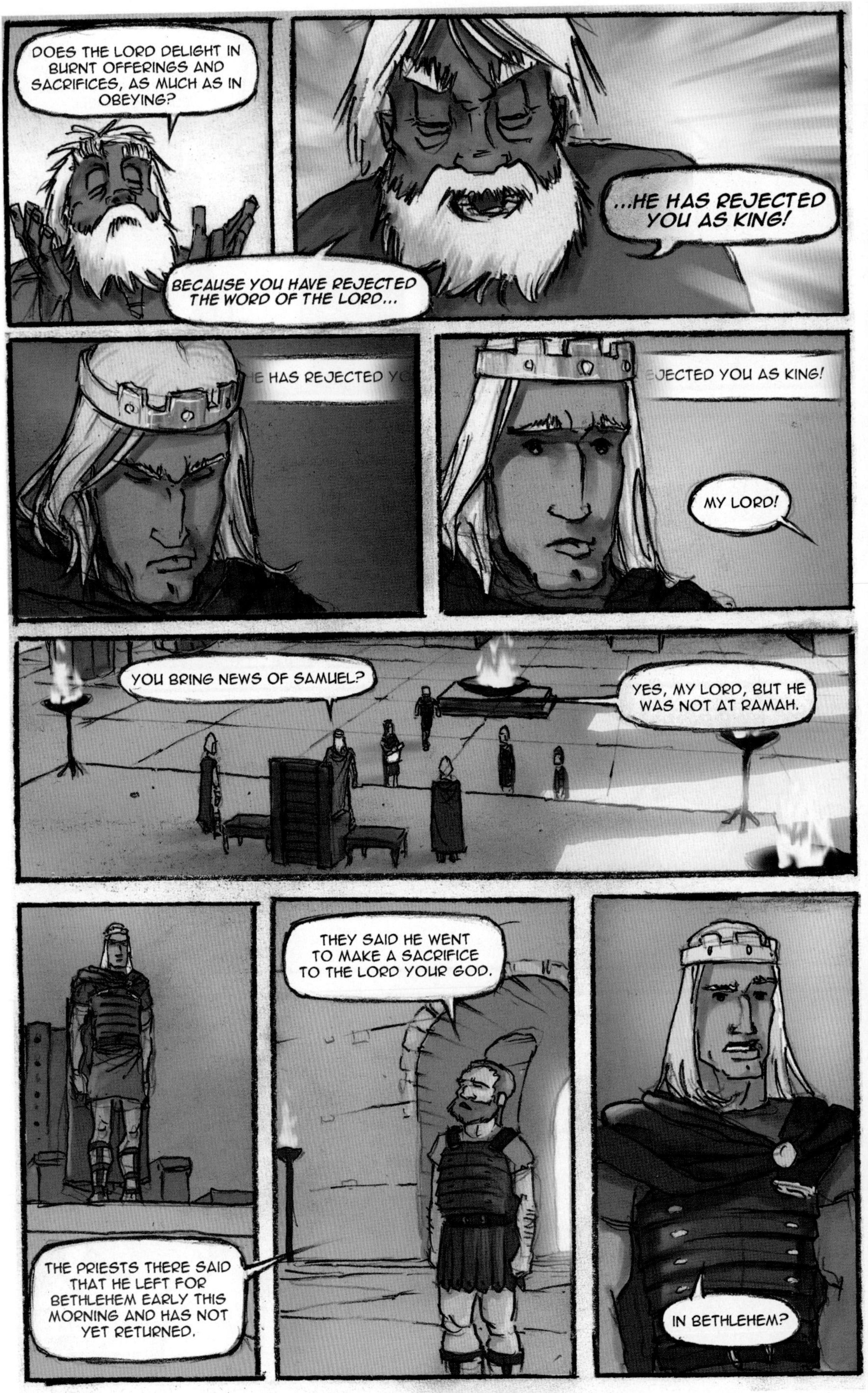
DOES THE LORD DELIGHT IN BURNT OFFERINGS AND SACRIFICES, AS MUCH AS IN OBEYING?
BECAUSE YOU HAVE REJECTED THE WORD OF THE LORD...
...HE HAS REJECTED YOU AS KING!
HE HAS REJECTED Y
EJECTED YOU AS KING!
MY LORD!
YOU BRING NEWS OF SAMUEL?
YES, MY LORD, BUT HE WAS NOT AT RAMAH.
THE PRIESTS THERE SAID THAT HE LEFT FOR BETHLEHEM EARLY THIS MORNING AND HAS NOT YET RETURNED.
THEY SAID HE WENT TO MAKE A SACRIFICE TO THE LORD YOUR GOD.
IN BETHLEHEM?

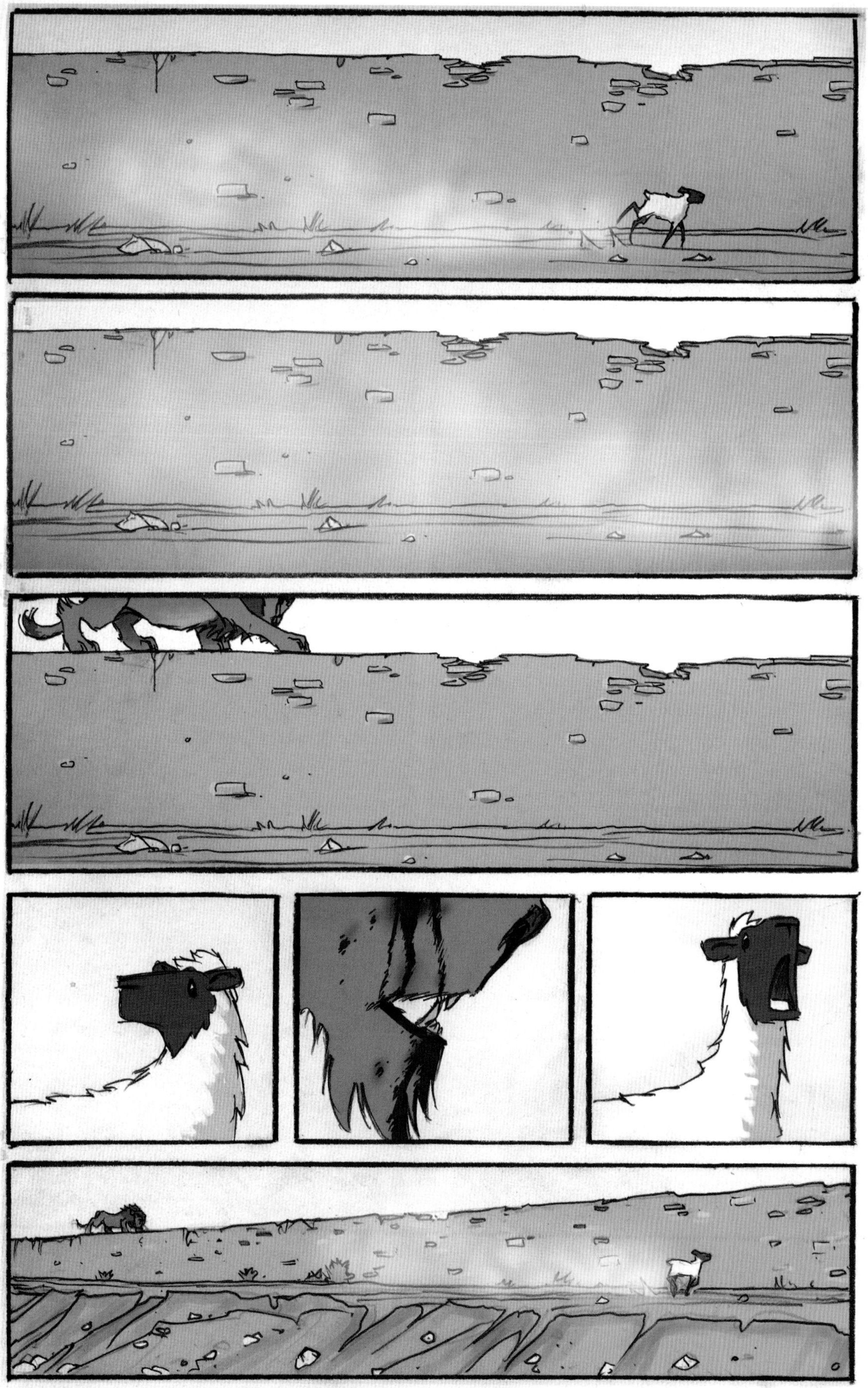

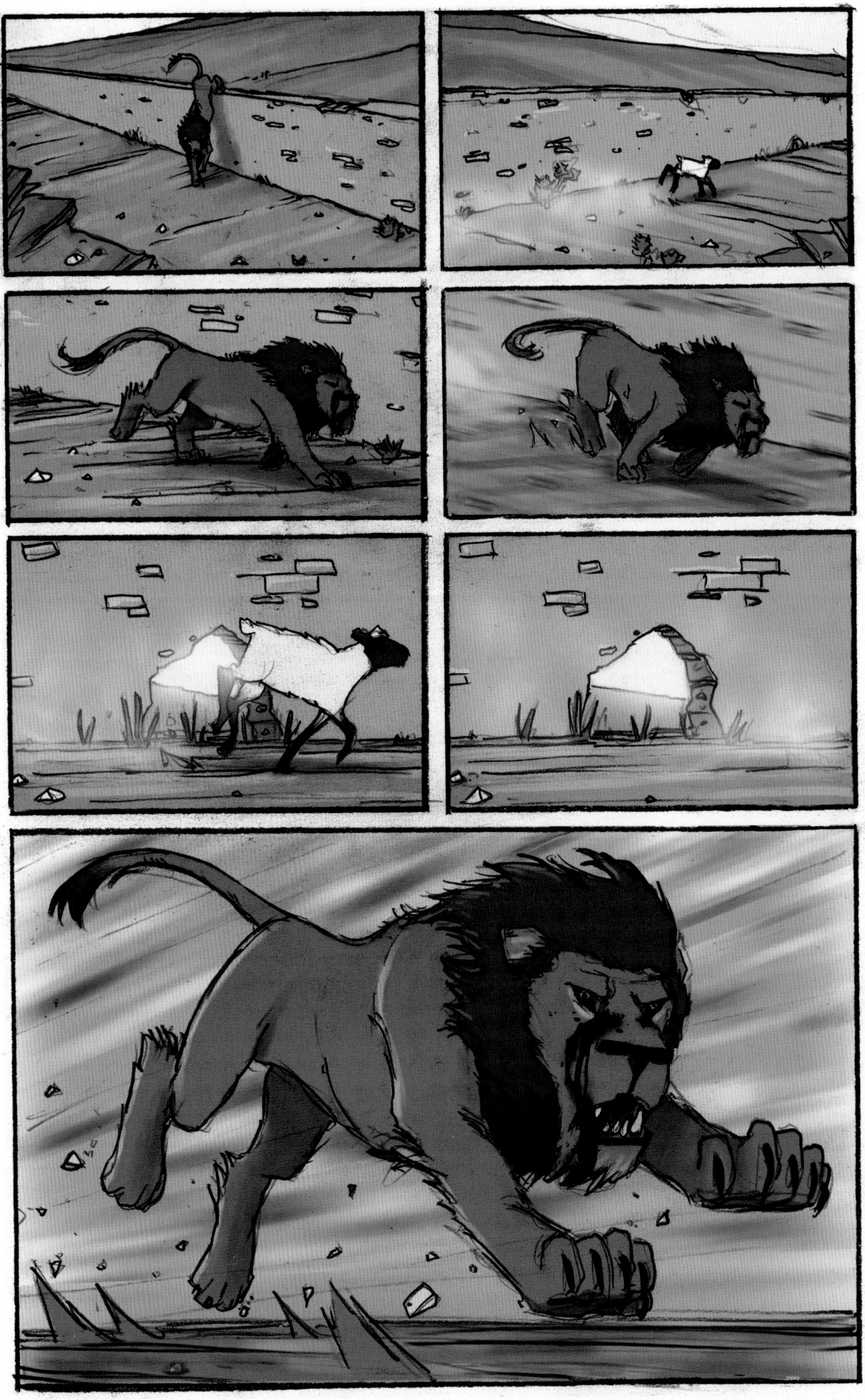

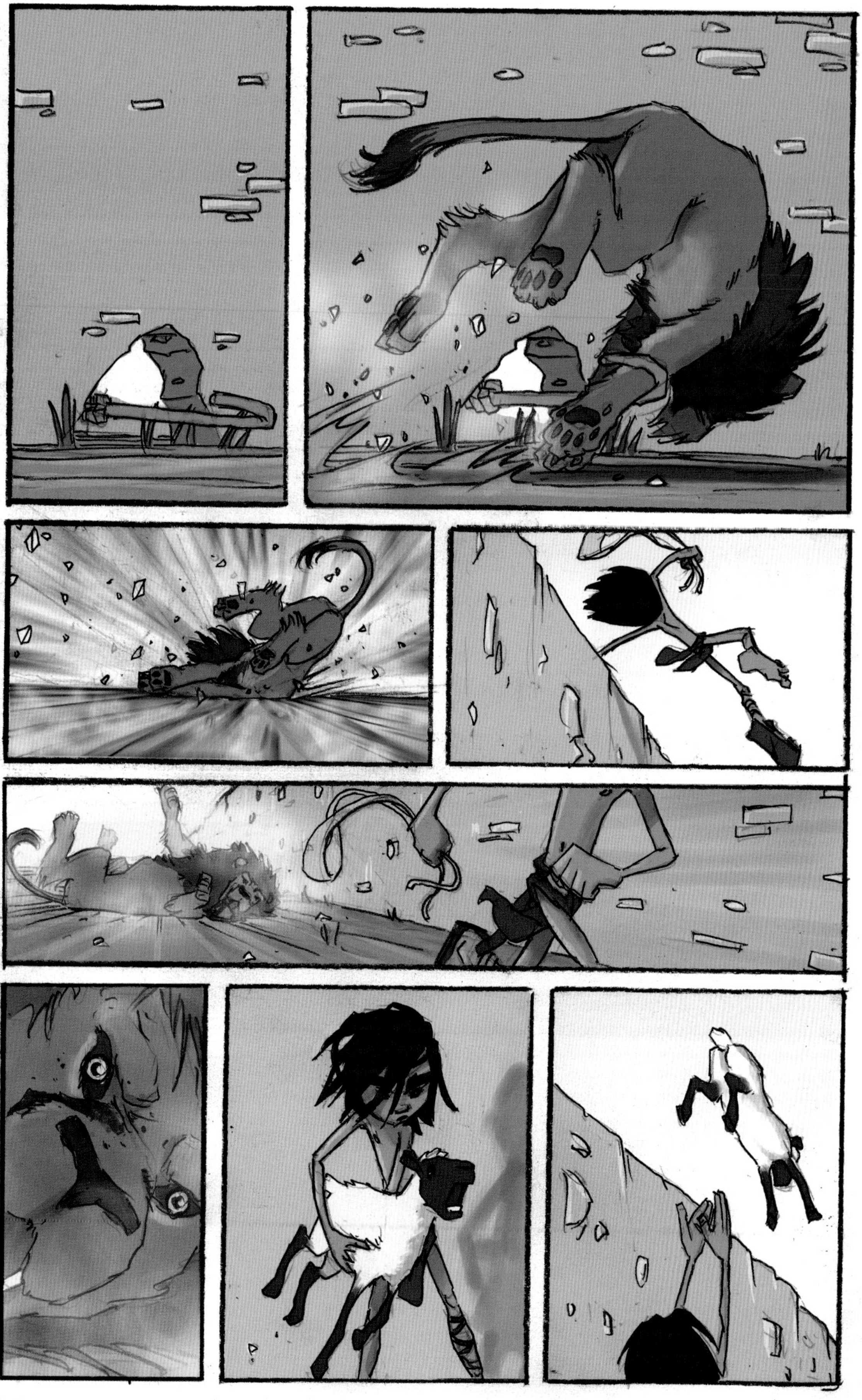

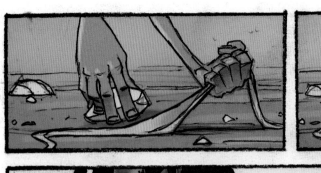

LISTEN TO MY PRAYER O GOD.

MY HEART IS IN ANGUISH WITHIN ME...

...THE TERRORS OF DEATH ASSAIL ME...

...FEAR AND TREMBLING HAVE BESET ME...

...HORROR HAS OVERWHELMED ME.

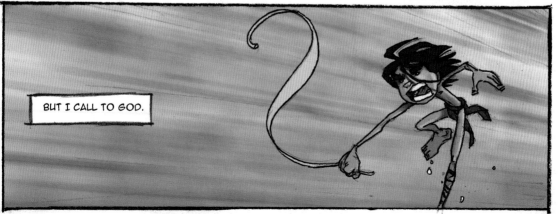

BUT I CALL TO GOD.

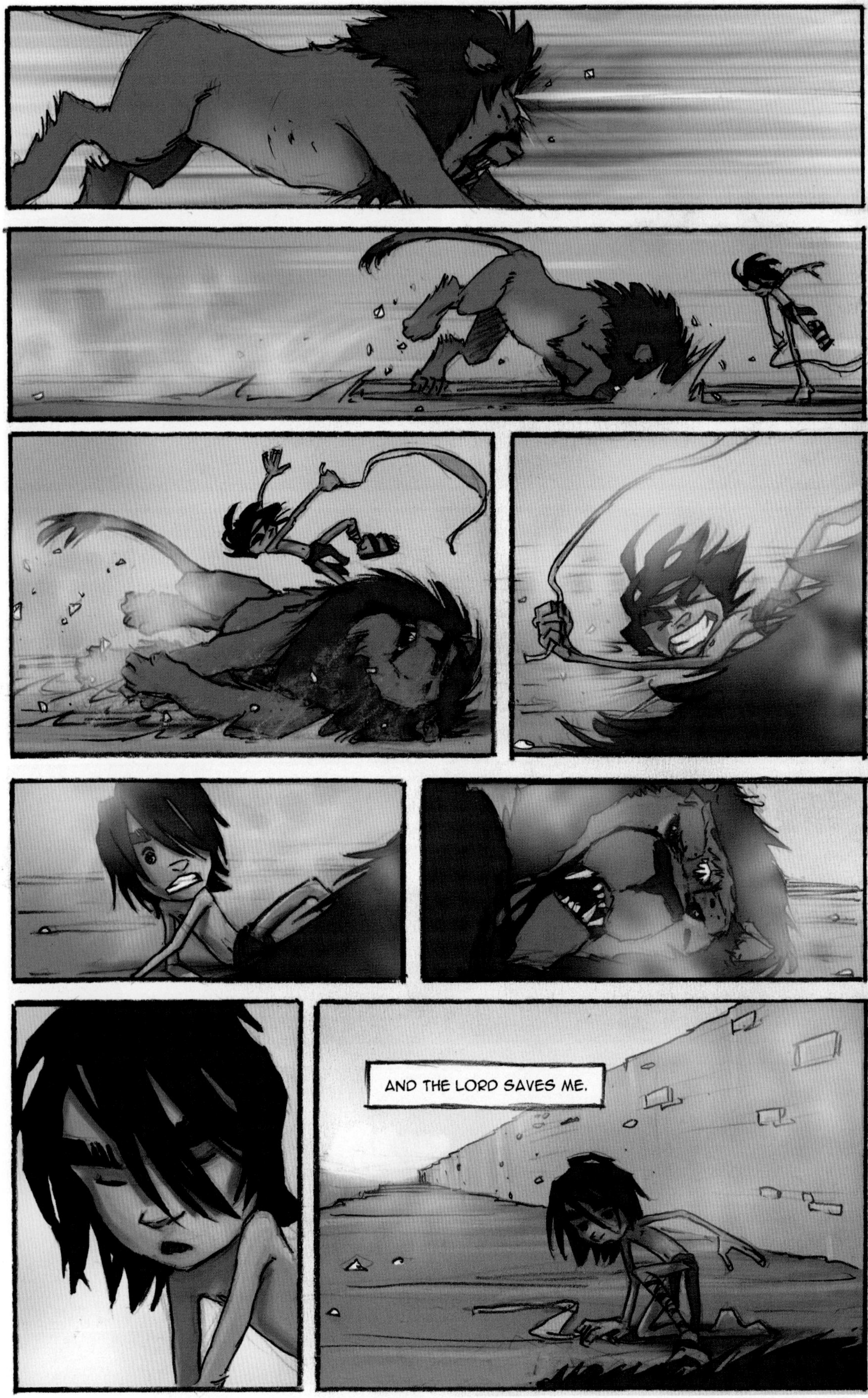
AND THE LORD SAVES ME.

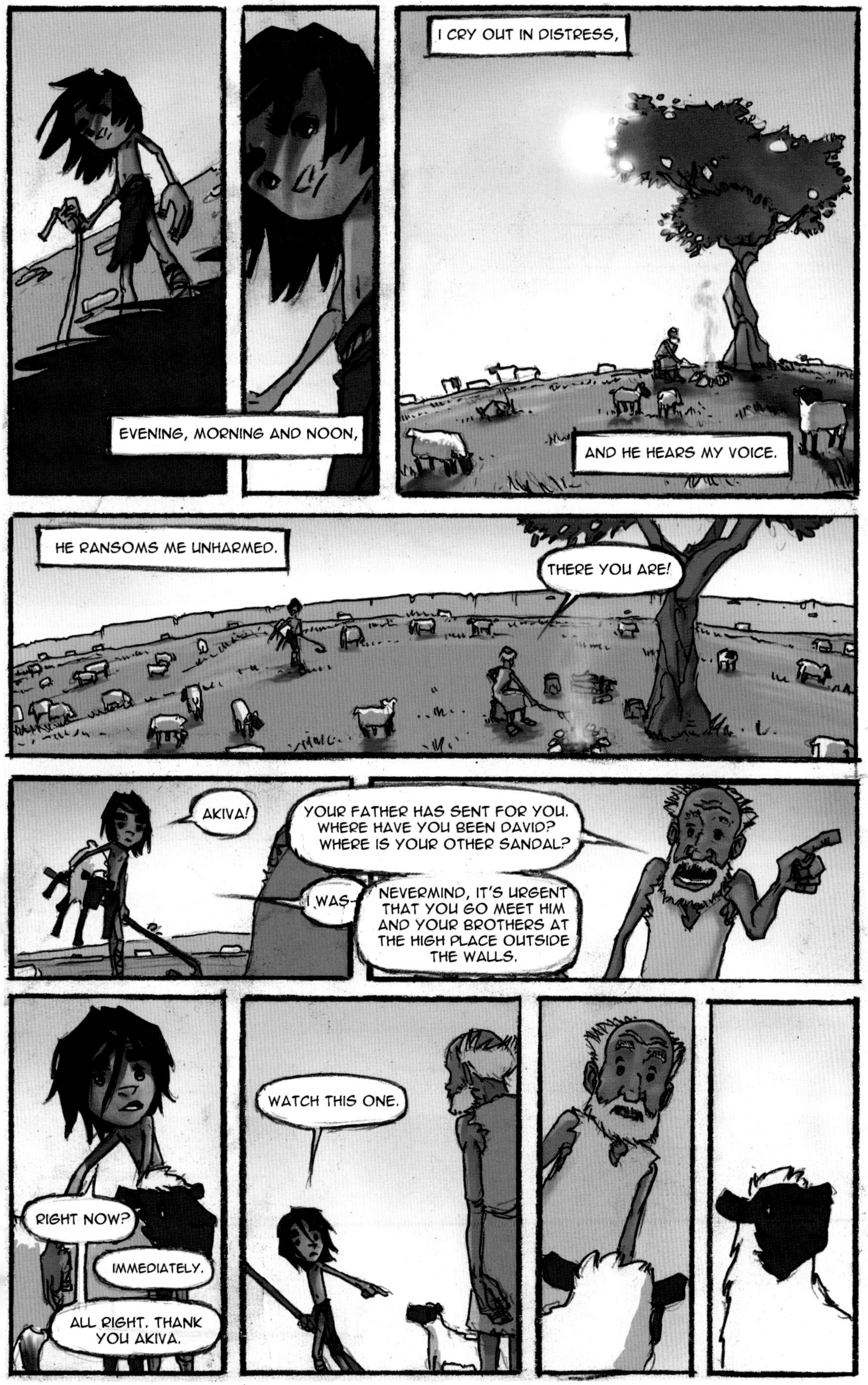
EVENING, MORNING AND NOON,
I CRY OUT IN DISTRESS,
AND HE HEARS MY VOICE.
HE RANSOMS ME UNHARMED.
THERE YOU ARE!
AKIVA!
YOUR FATHER HAS SENT FOR YOU. WHERE HAVE YOU BEEN DAVID? WHERE IS YOUR OTHER SANDAL?
I WAS-
NEVERMIND, IT'S URGENT THAT YOU GO MEET HIM AND YOUR BROTHERS AT THE HIGH PLACE OUTSIDE THE WALLS.
RIGHT NOW?
IMMEDIATELY.
ALL RIGHT. THANK YOU AKIVA.
WATCH THIS ONE.

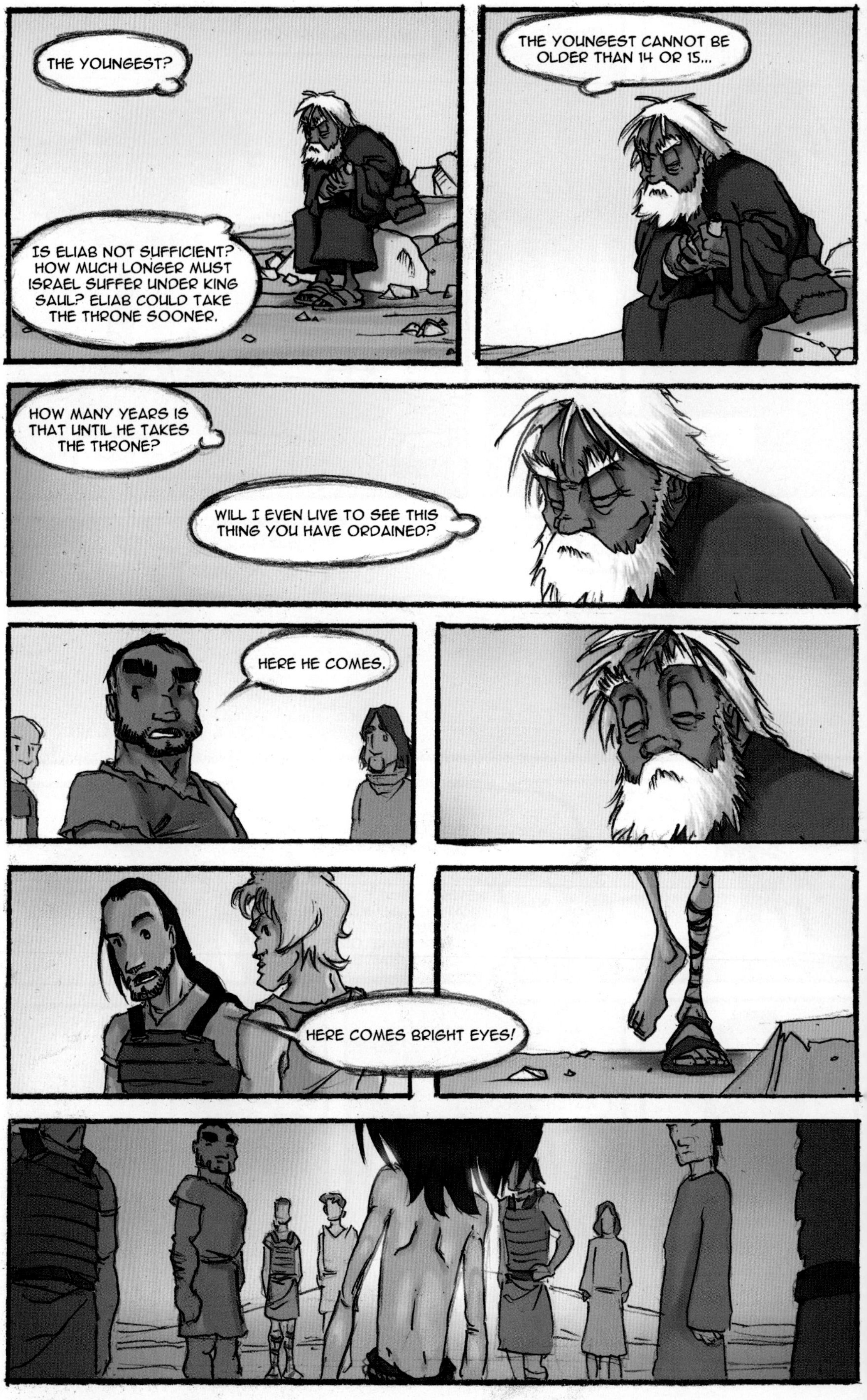
THE YOUNGEST?
IS ELIAB NOT SUFFICIENT? HOW MUCH LONGER MUST ISRAEL SUFFER UNDER KING SAUL? ELIAB COULD TAKE THE THRONE SOONER.
THE YOUNGEST CANNOT BE OLDER THAN 14 OR 15...
HOW MANY YEARS IS THAT UNTIL HE TAKES THE THRONE?
WILL I EVEN LIVE TO SEE THIS THING YOU HAVE ORDAINED?
HERE HE COMES.
HERE COMES BRIGHT EYES!

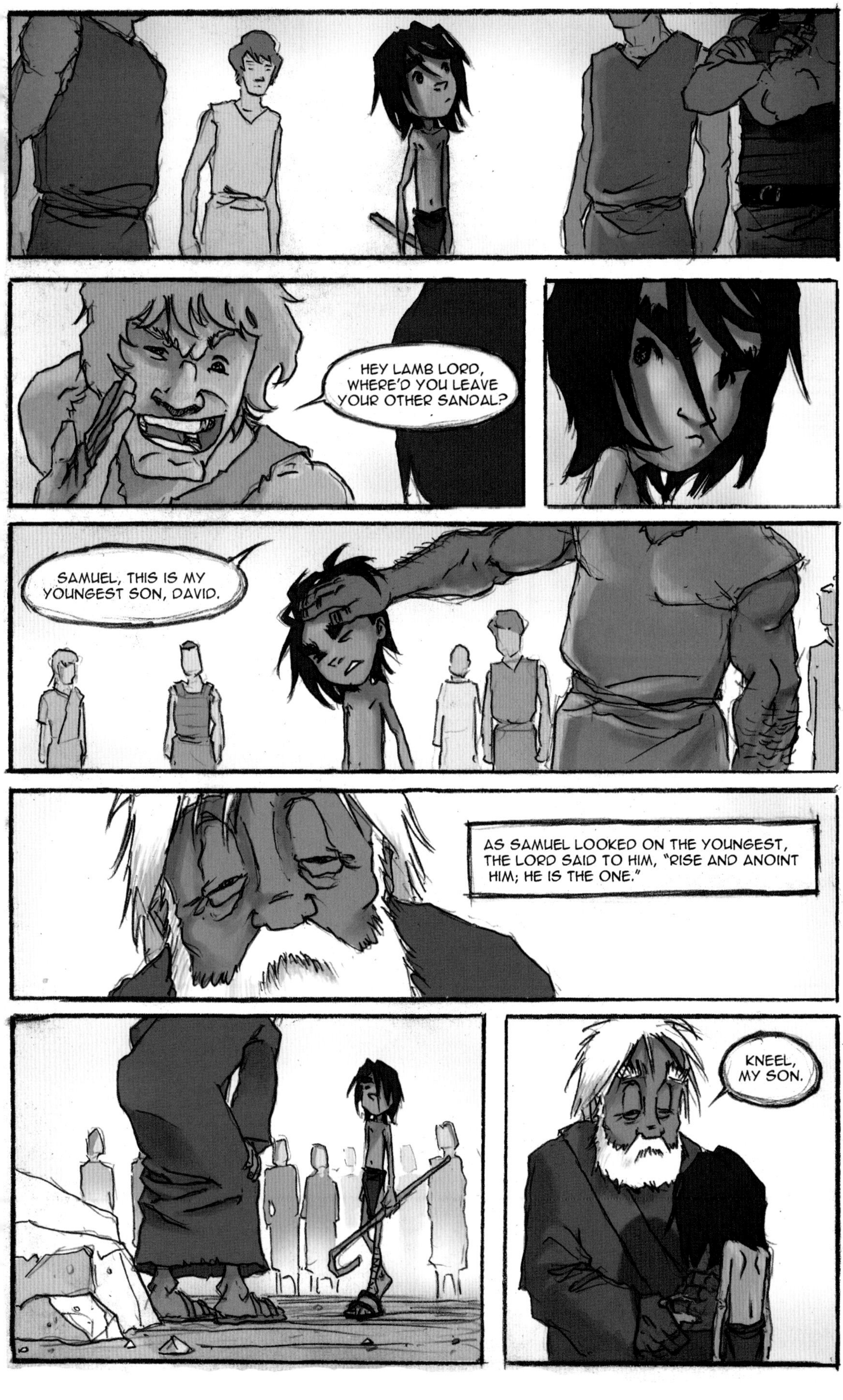
HEY LAMB LORD, WHERE'D YOU LEAVE YOUR OTHER SANDAL?
SAMUEL, THIS IS MY YOUNGEST SON, DAVID.
AS SAMUEL LOOKED ON THE YOUNGEST, THE LORD SAID TO HIM, "RISE AND ANOINT HIM; HE IS THE ONE."
KNEEL, MY SON.

WHAT'S GOING ON?

IS THIS A JOKE?

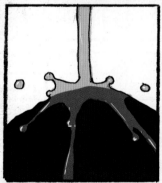

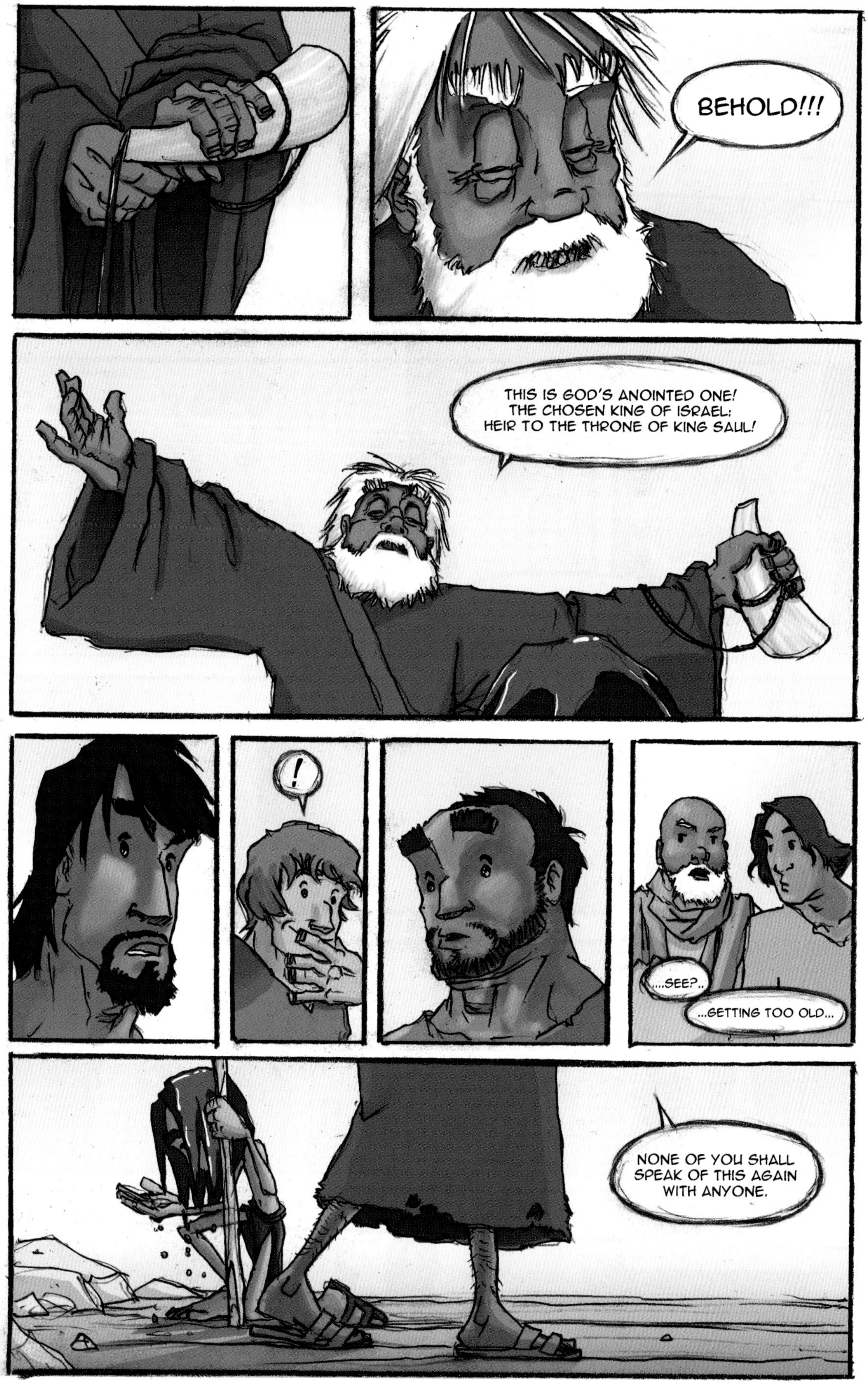
BEHOLD!!!
THIS IS GOD'S ANOINTED ONE! THE CHOSEN KING OF ISRAEL: HEIR TO THE THRONE OF KING SAUL!
!
...SEE?..
...GETTING TOO OLD...
NONE OF YOU SHALL SPEAK OF THIS AGAIN WITH ANYONE.

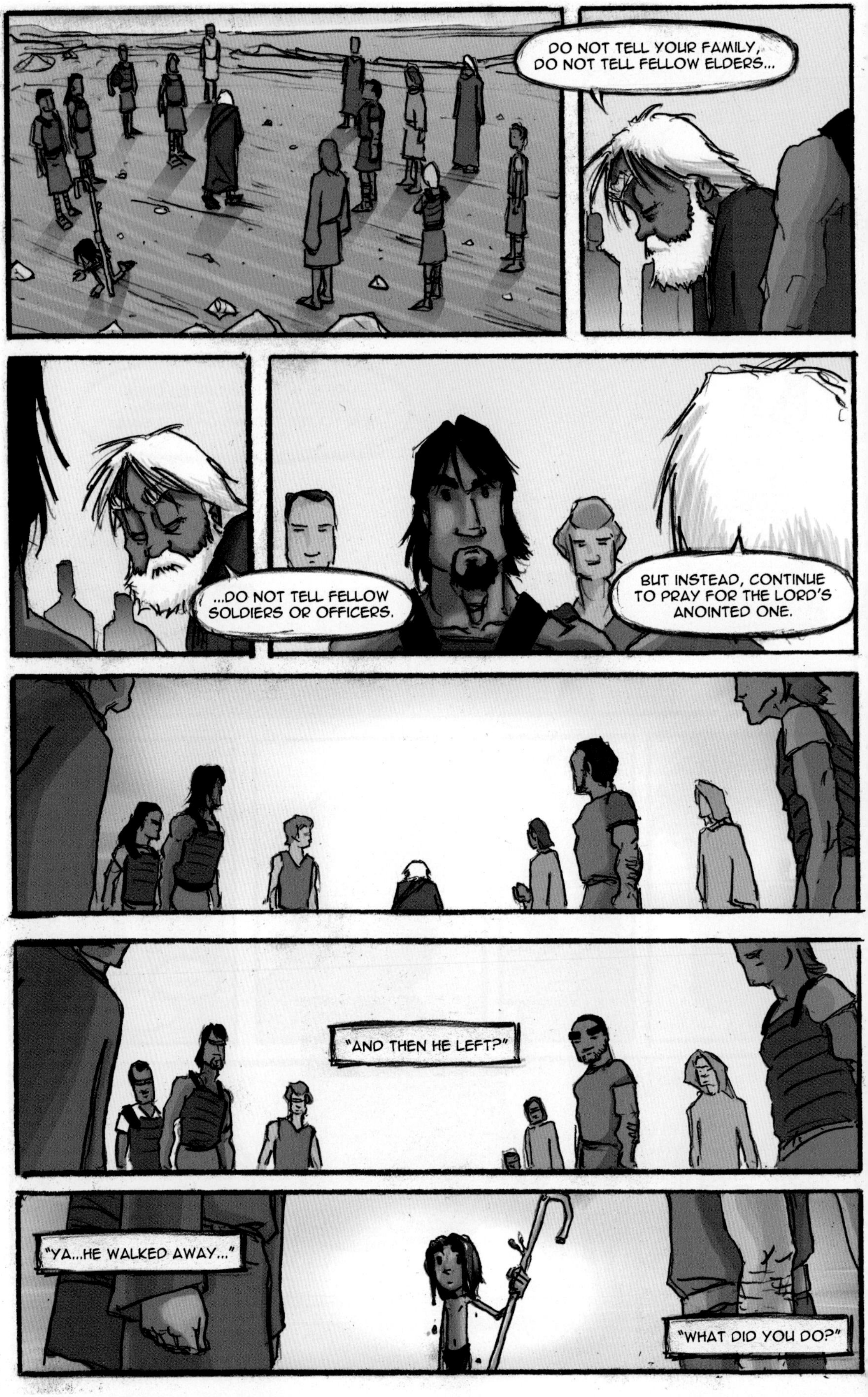
DO NOT TELL YOUR FAMILY, DO NOT TELL FELLOW ELDERS...
...DO NOT TELL FELLOW SOLDIERS OR OFFICERS.
BUT INSTEAD, CONTINUE TO PRAY FOR THE LORD'S ANOINTED ONE.
"AND THEN HE LEFT?"
"YA...HE WALKED AWAY..."
"WHAT DID YOU DO?"

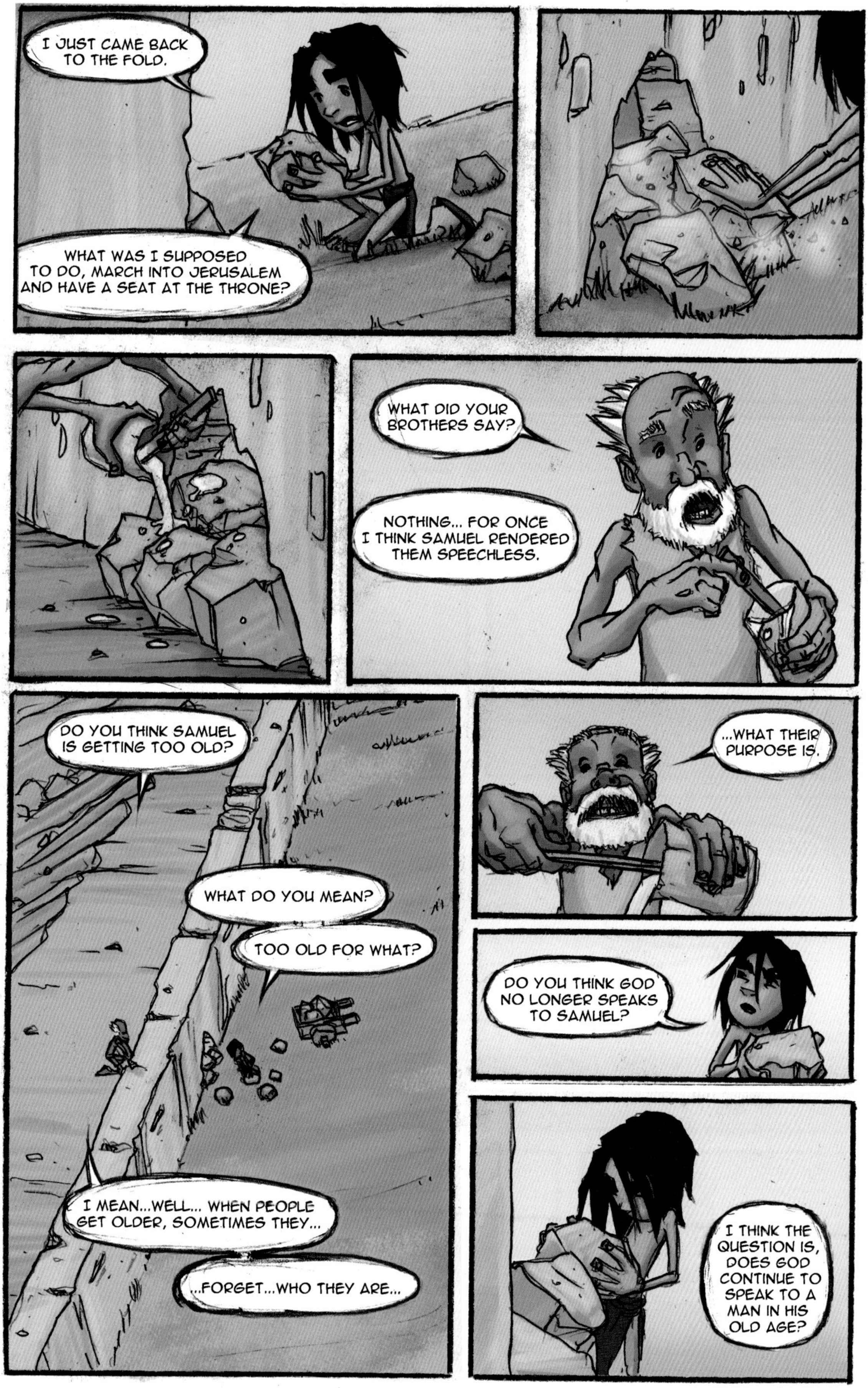
I JUST CAME BACK TO THE FOLD.
WHAT WAS I SUPPOSED TO DO, MARCH INTO JERUSALEM AND HAVE A SEAT AT THE THRONE?
WHAT DID YOUR BROTHERS SAY?
NOTHING... FOR ONCE I THINK SAMUEL RENDERED THEM SPEECHLESS.
DO YOU THINK SAMUEL IS GETTING TOO OLD?
WHAT DO YOU MEAN?
TOO OLD FOR WHAT?
I MEAN...WELL... WHEN PEOPLE GET OLDER, SOMETIMES THEY...
...FORGET...WHO THEY ARE...
...WHAT THEIR PURPOSE IS.
DO YOU THINK GOD NO LONGER SPEAKS TO SAMUEL?
I THINK THE QUESTION IS, DOES GOD CONTINUE TO SPEAK TO A MAN IN HIS OLD AGE?

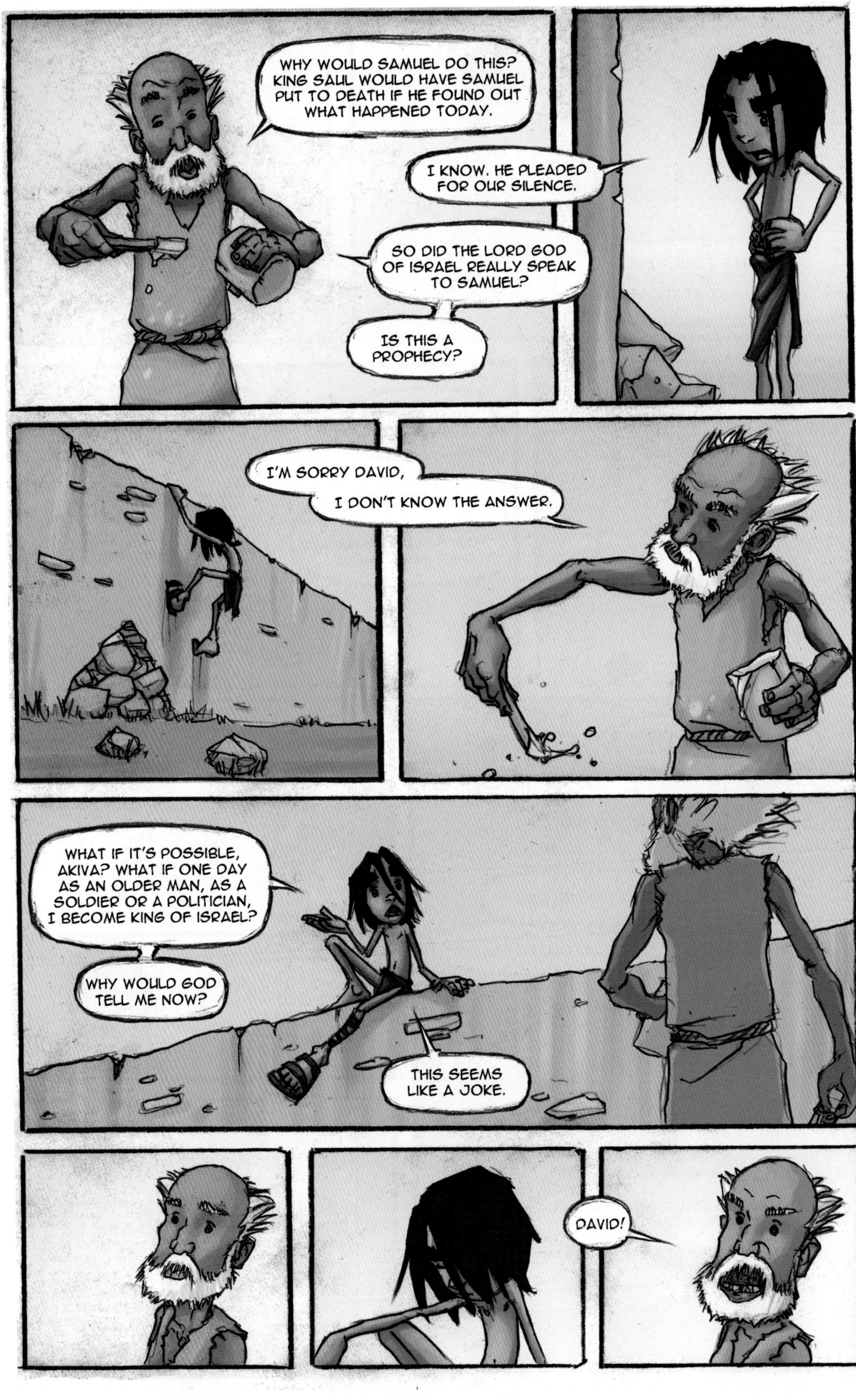

WHY WOULD SAMUEL DO THIS? KING SAUL WOULD HAVE SAMUEL PUT TO DEATH IF HE FOUND OUT WHAT HAPPENED TODAY.
I KNOW. HE PLEADED FOR OUR SILENCE.
SO DID THE LORD GOD OF ISRAEL REALLY SPEAK TO SAMUEL?
IS THIS A PROPHECY?
I'M SORRY DAVID,
I DON'T KNOW THE ANSWER.
WHAT IF IT'S POSSIBLE, AKIVA? WHAT IF ONE DAY AS AN OLDER MAN, AS A SOLDIER OR A POLITICIAN, I BECOME KING OF ISRAEL?
WHY WOULD GOD TELL ME NOW?
THIS SEEMS LIKE A JOKE.
DAVID!

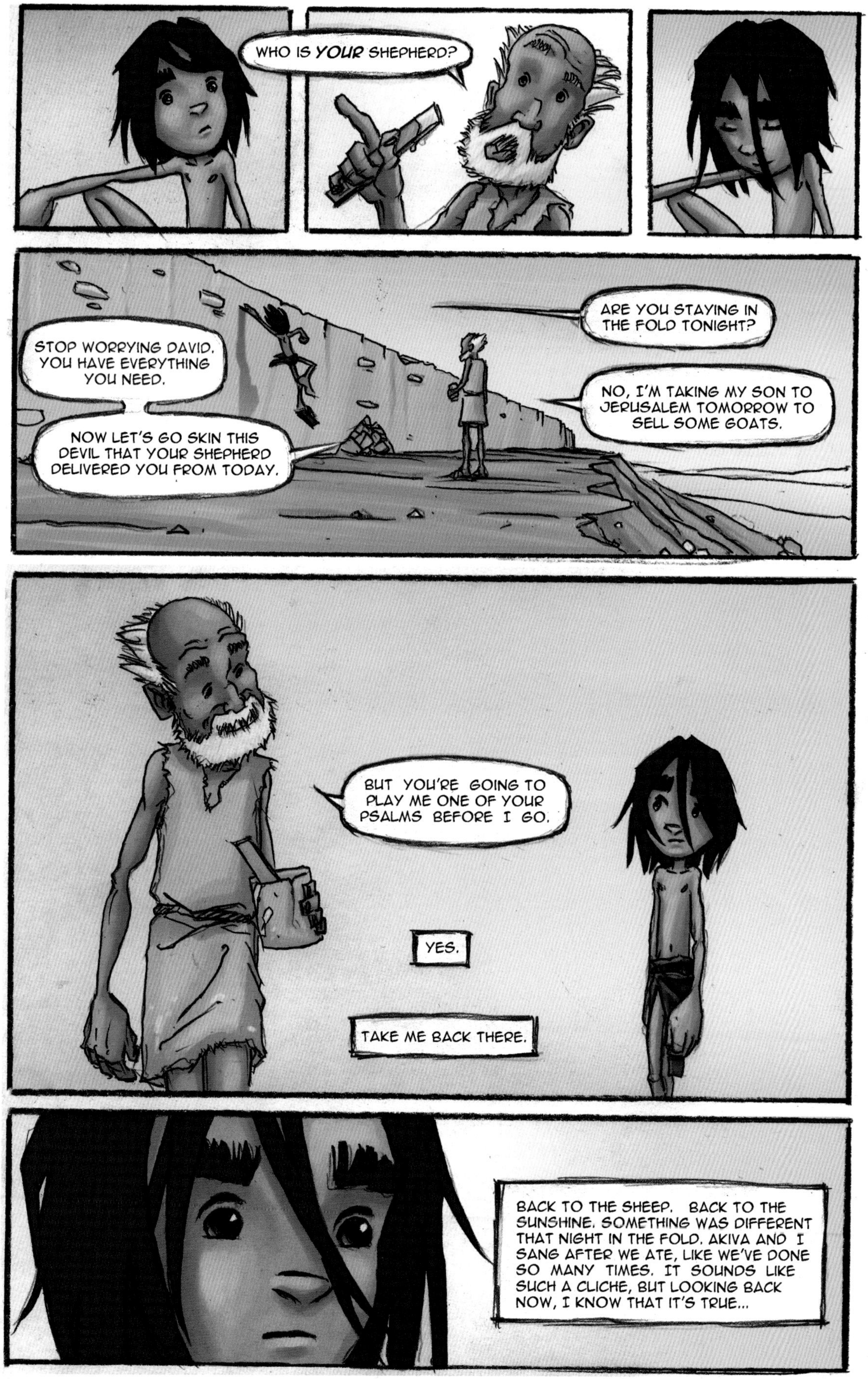
WHO IS YOUR SHEPHERD?
ARE YOU STAYING IN THE FOLD TONIGHT?
STOP WORRYING DAVID. YOU HAVE EVERYTHING YOU NEED.
NO, I'M TAKING MY SON TO JERUSALEM TOMORROW TO SELL SOME GOATS.
NOW LET'S GO SKIN THIS DEVIL THAT YOUR SHEPHERD DELIVERED YOU FROM TODAY.
BUT YOU'RE GOING TO PLAY ME ONE OF YOUR PSALMS BEFORE I GO.
YES.
TAKE ME BACK THERE.
BACK TO THE SHEEP. BACK TO THE SUNSHINE. SOMETHING WAS DIFFERENT THAT NIGHT IN THE FOLD. AKIVA AND I SANG AFTER WE ATE, LIKE WE'VE DONE SO MANY TIMES. IT SOUNDS LIKE SUCH A CLICHE, BUT LOOKING BACK NOW, I KNOW THAT IT'S TRUE...

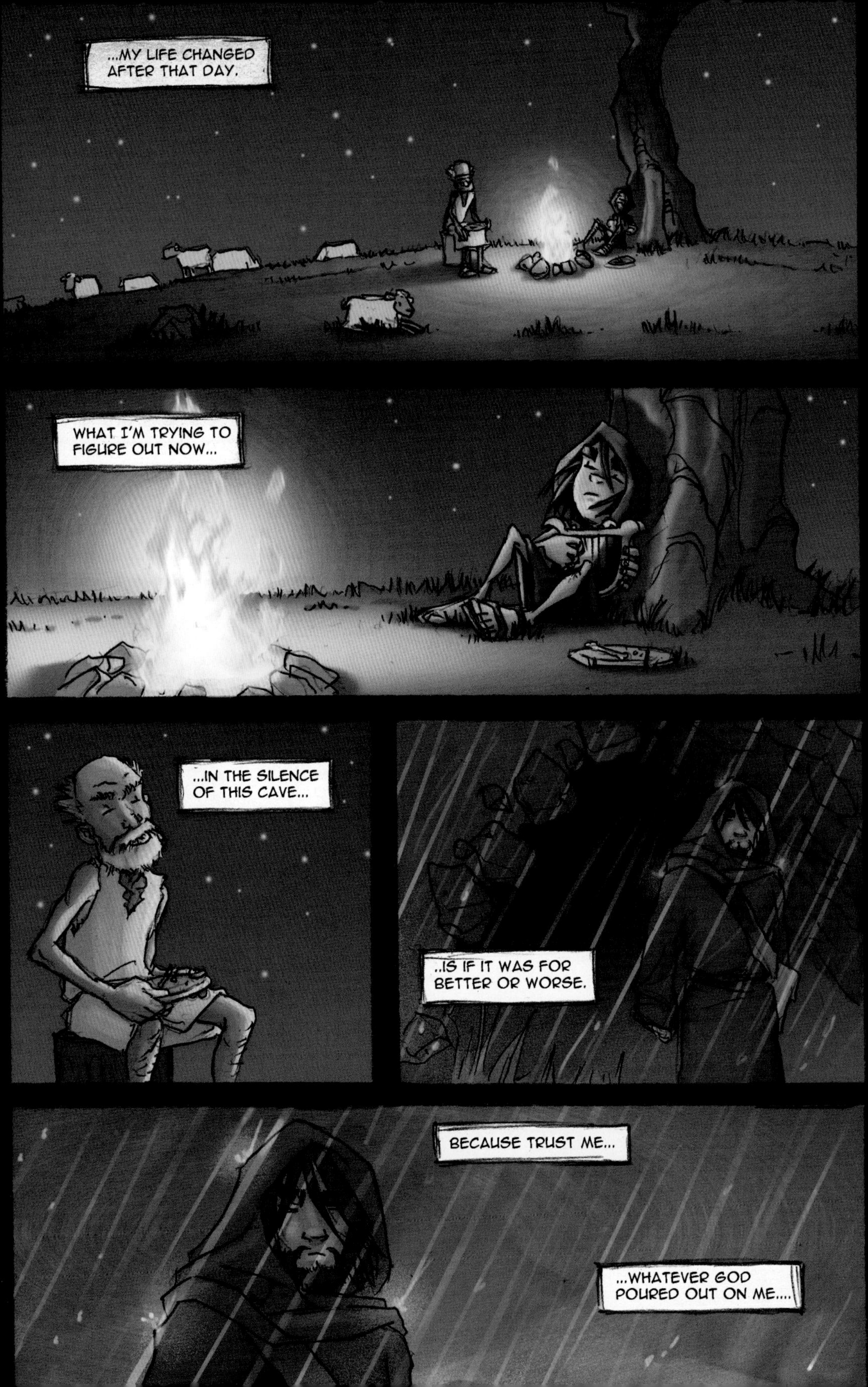
...MY LIFE CHANGED AFTER THAT DAY.
WHAT I'M TRYING TO FIGURE OUT NOW...
...IN THE SILENCE OF THIS CAVE...
...IS IF IT WAS FOR BETTER OR WORSE.
BECAUSE TRUST ME...
...WHATEVER GOD POURED OUT ON ME....

...WAS CLEARLY REMOVED FROM SAUL.

AND IT WAS REPLACED WITH SOMETHING EVIL.

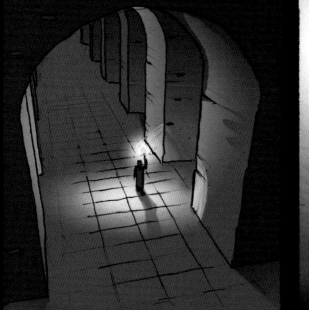

SAUL!

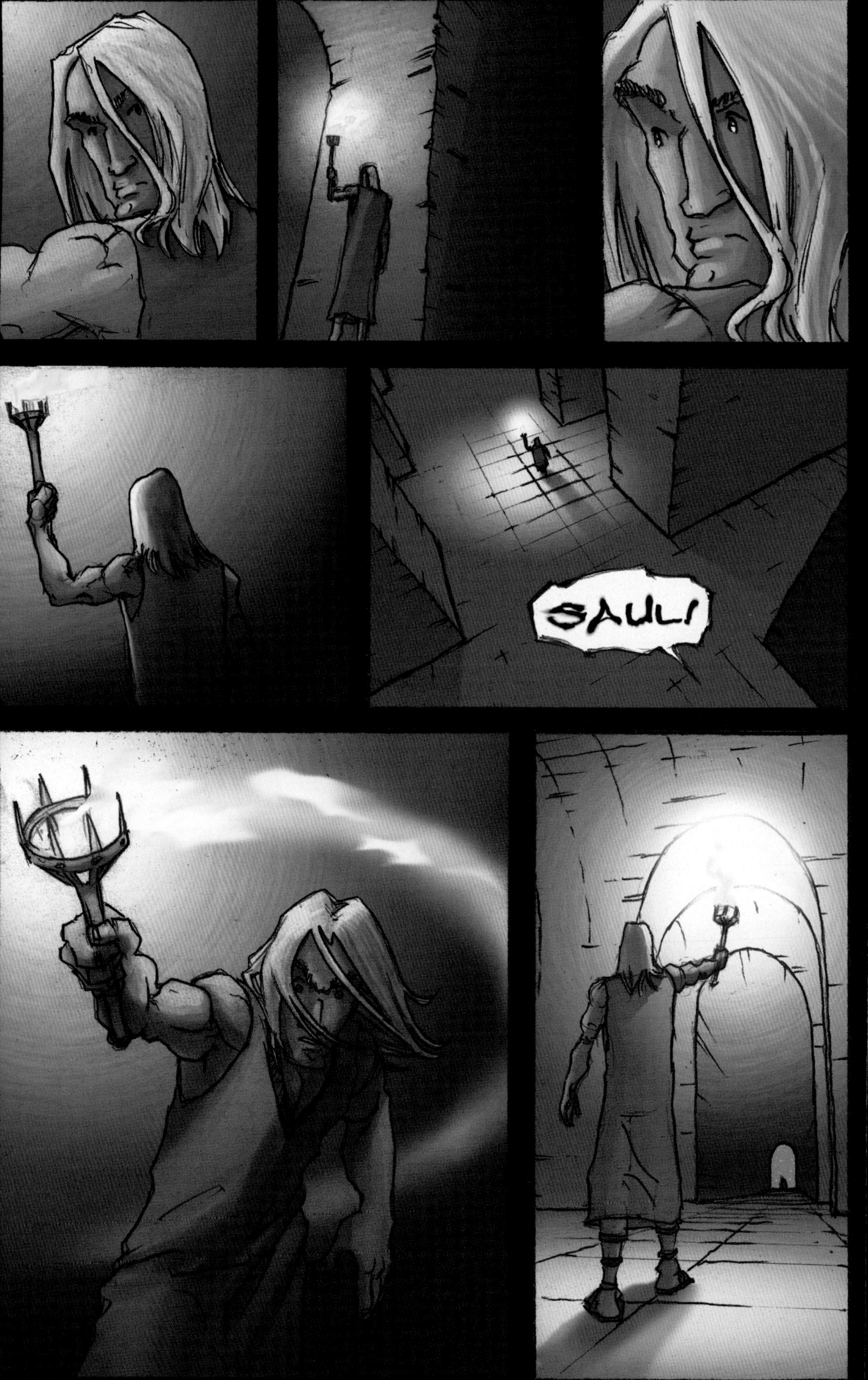
SAUL!

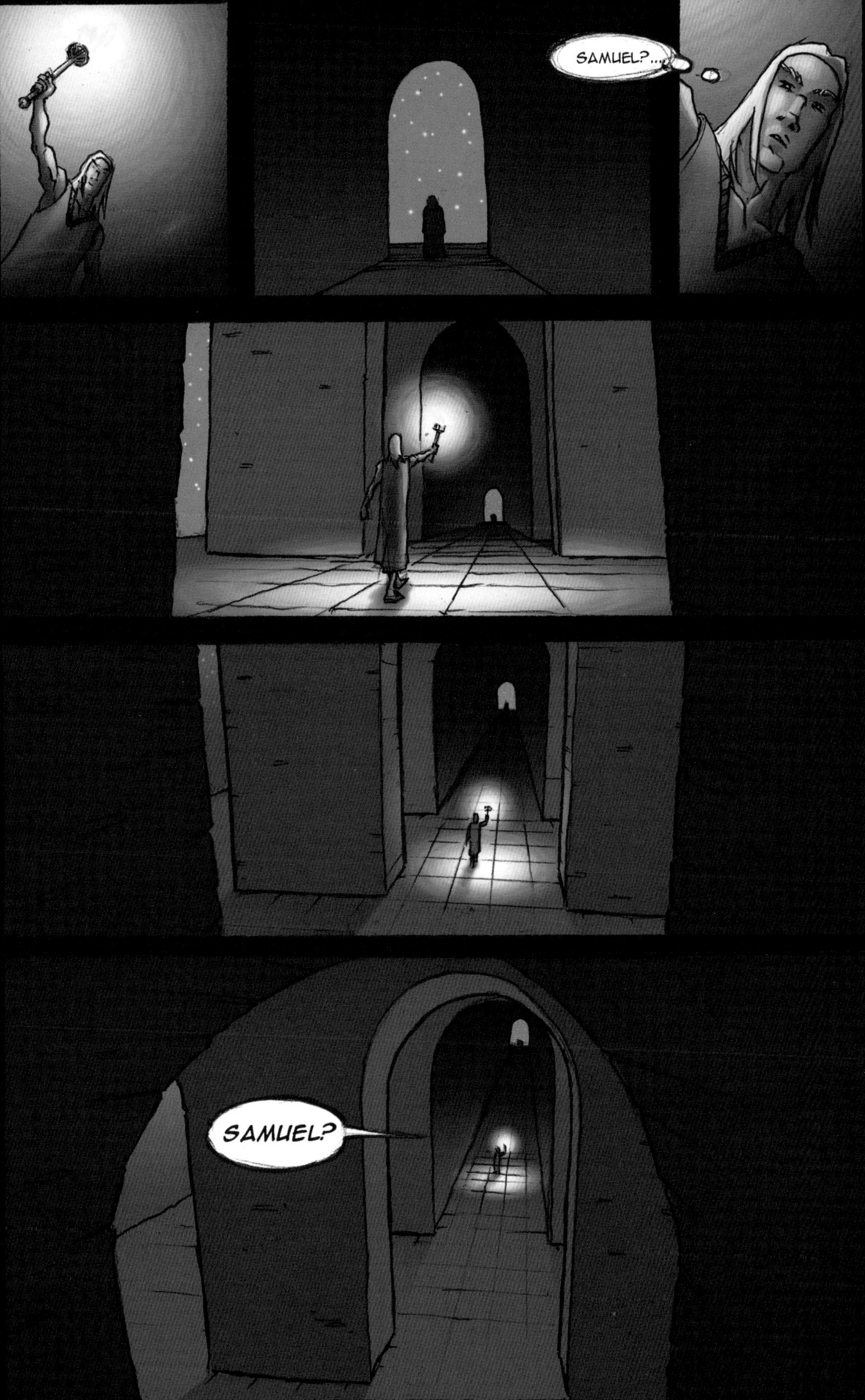
SAMUEL?...
SAMUEL?

CHAPTER 3

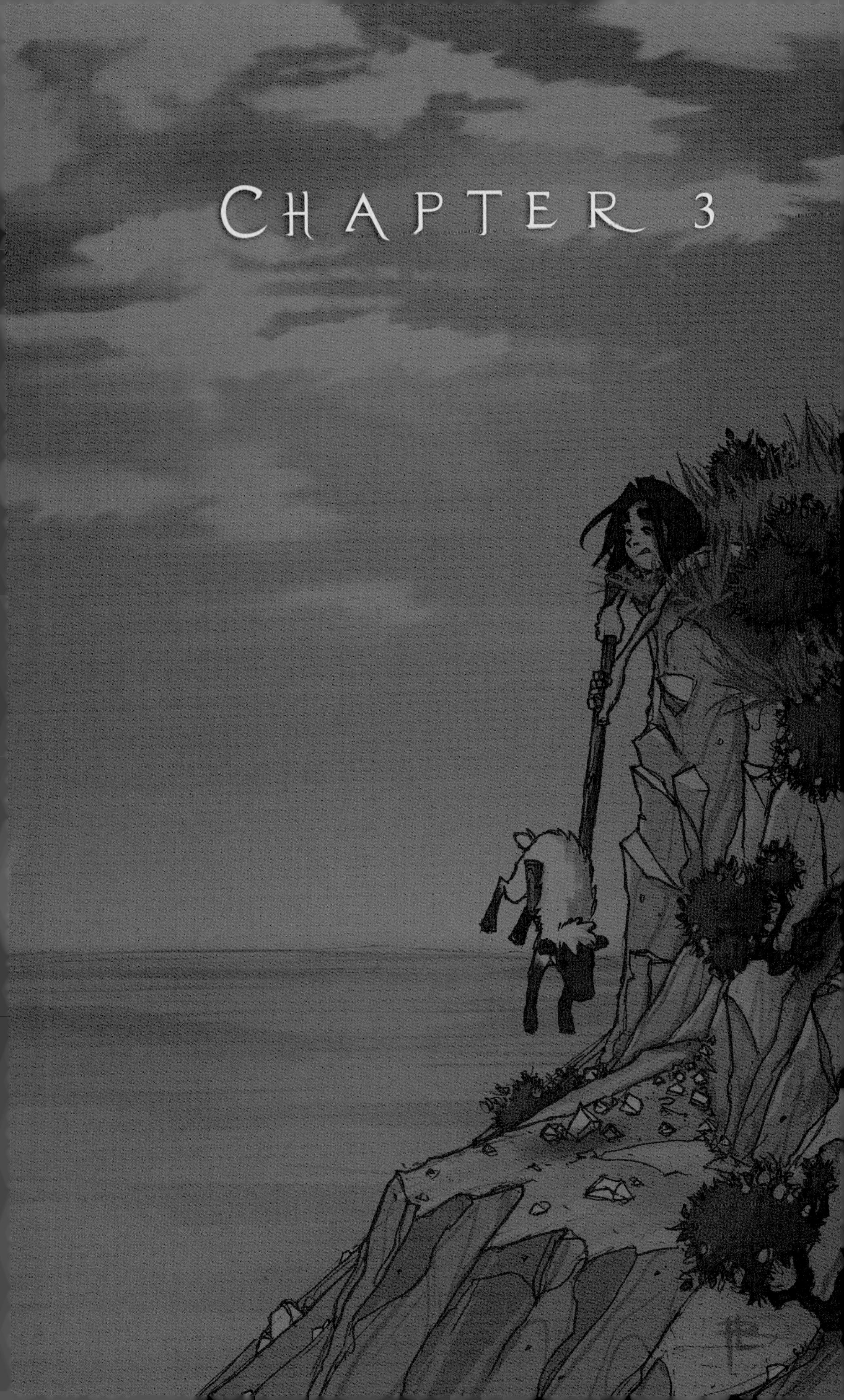

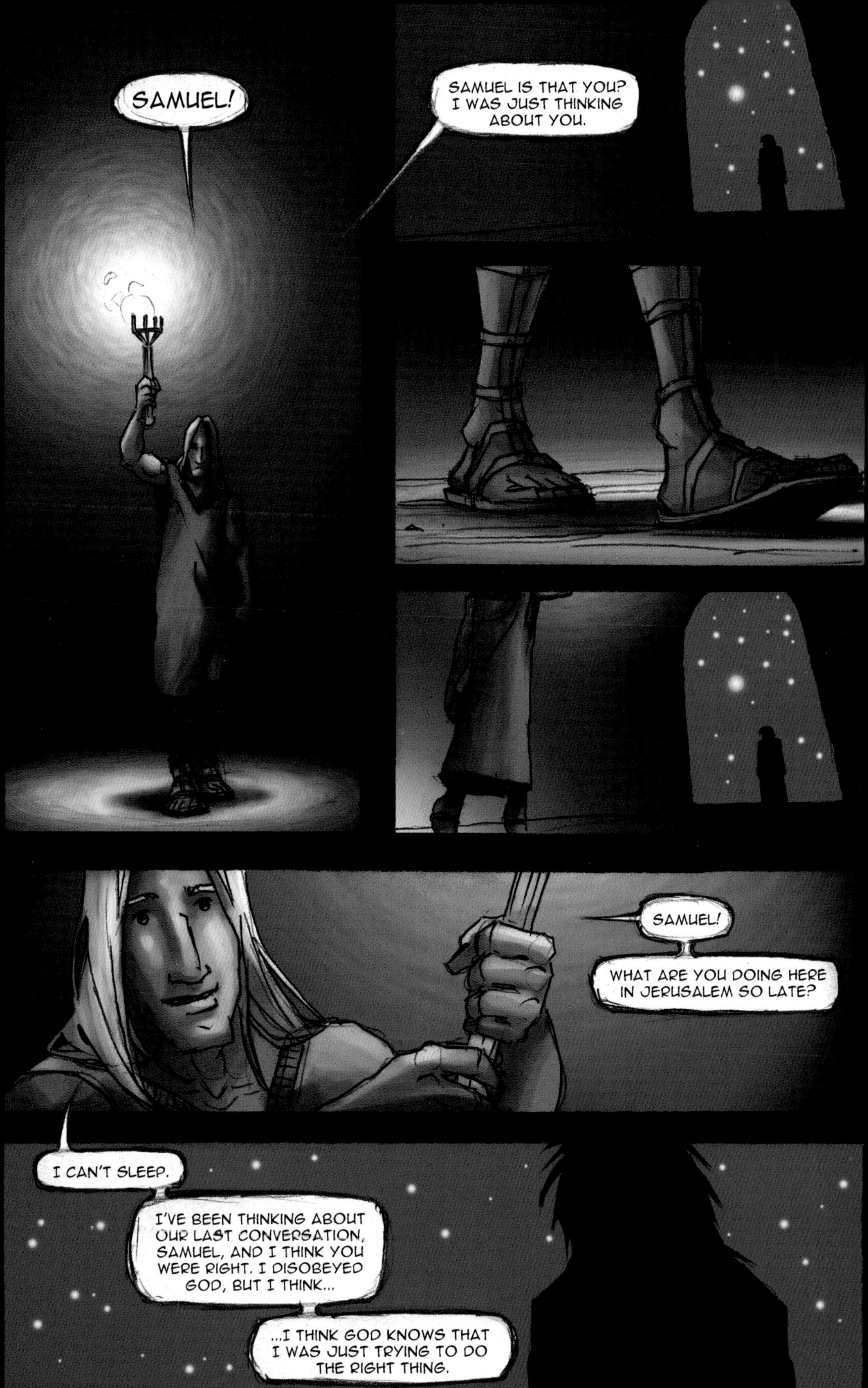
SAMUEL!
SAMUEL IS THAT YOU? I WAS JUST THINKING ABOUT YOU.
SAMUEL!
WHAT ARE YOU DOING HERE IN JERUSALEM SO LATE?
I CAN'T SLEEP.
I'VE BEEN THINKING ABOUT OUR LAST CONVERSATION, SAMUEL, AND I THINK YOU WERE RIGHT. I DISOBEYED GOD, BUT I THINK...
...I THINK GOD KNOWS THAT I WAS JUST TRYING TO DO THE RIGHT THING.

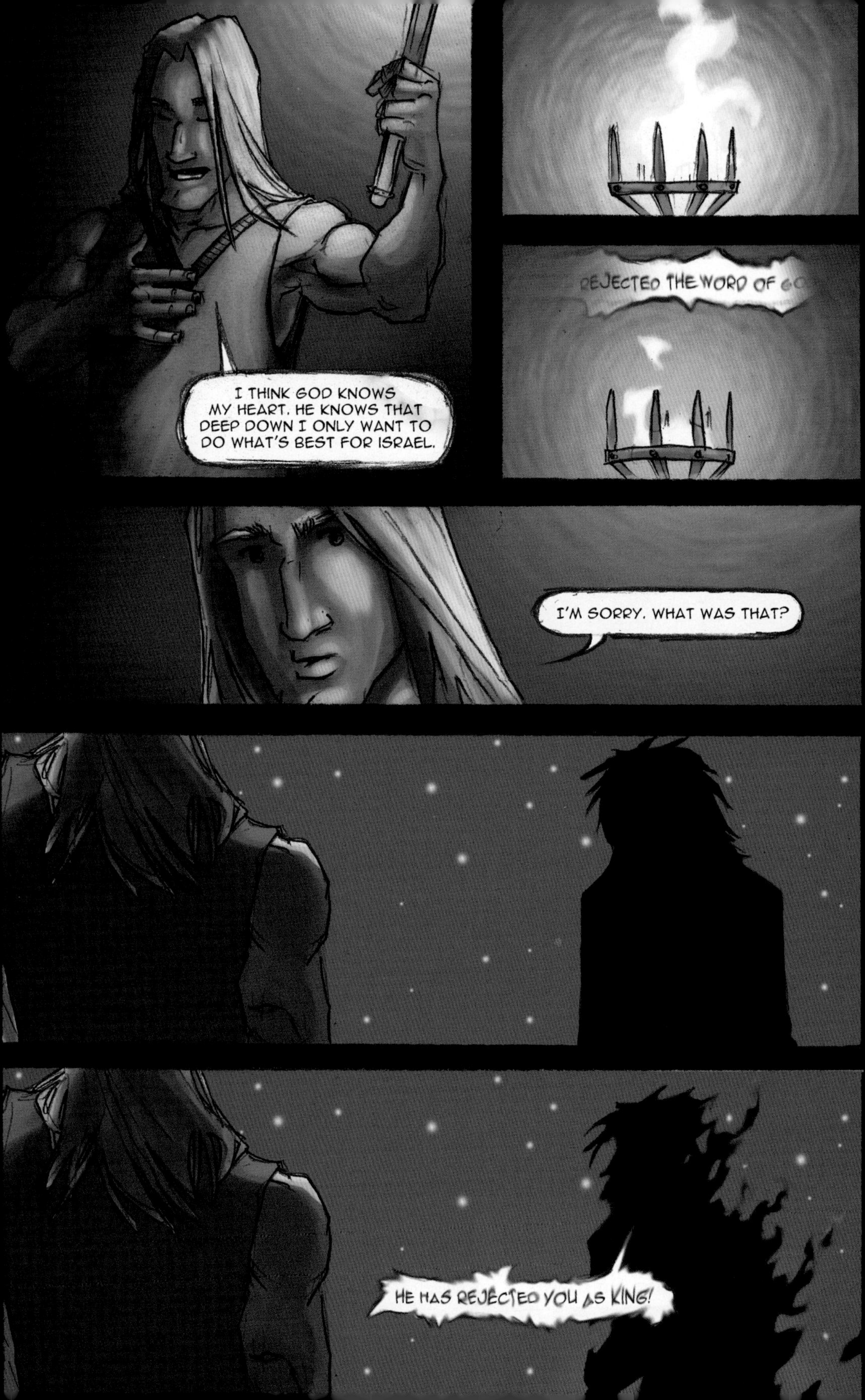
I THINK GOD KNOWS MY HEART. HE KNOWS THAT DEEP DOWN I ONLY WANT TO DO WHAT'S BEST FOR ISRAEL.
REJECTED THE WORD OF
I'M SORRY. WHAT WAS THAT?
HE HAS REJECTED YOU AS KING!

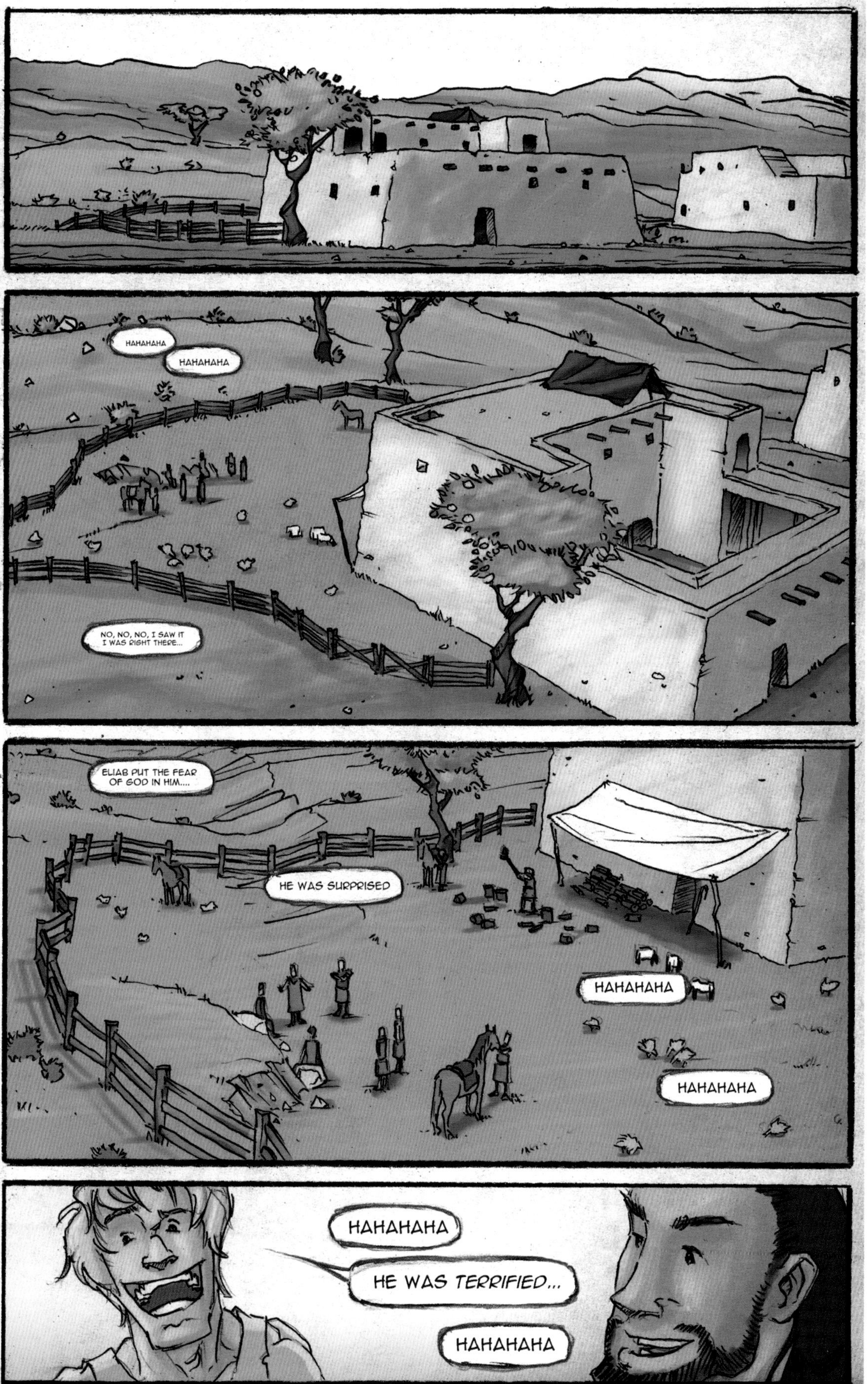
HAHAHAHA
HAHAHAHA
NO, NO, NO, I SAW IT I WAS RIGHT THERE...
ELIAB PUT THE FEAR OF GOD IN HIM....
HE WAS SURPRISED
HAHAHAHA
HAHAHAHA
HAHAHAHA
HE WAS TERRIFIED...
HAHAHAHA

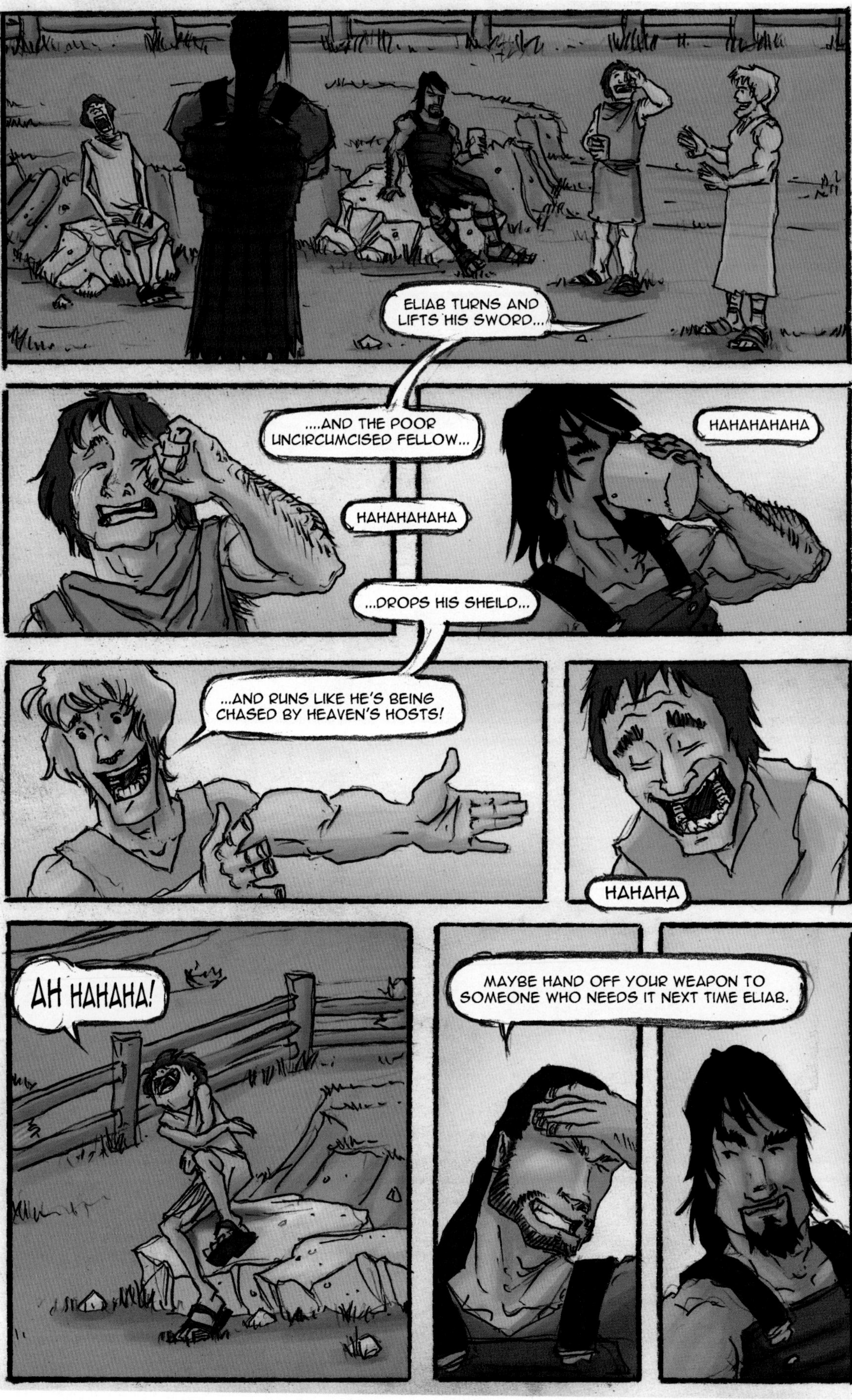
ELIAB TURNS AND LIFTS HIS SWORD...
....AND THE POOR UNCIRCUMCISED FELLOW...
HAHAHAHAHA
HAHAHAHAHA
...DROPS HIS SHEILD...
...AND RUNS LIKE HE'S BEING CHASED BY HEAVEN'S HOSTS!
HAHAHA
AH HAHAHA!
MAYBE HAND OFF YOUR WEAPON TO SOMEONE WHO NEEDS IT NEXT TIME ELIAB.

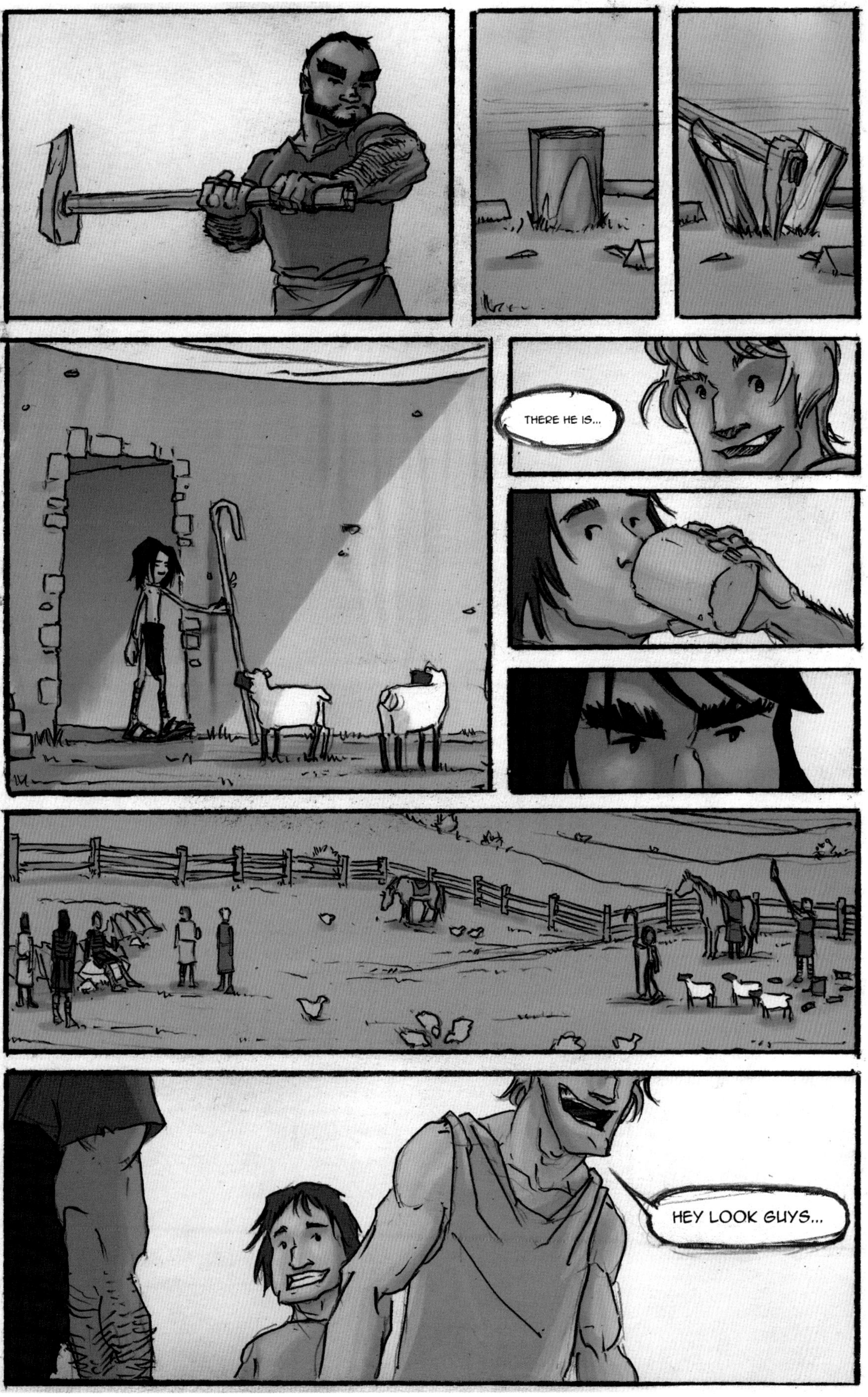
THERE HE IS...
HEY LOOK GUYS...

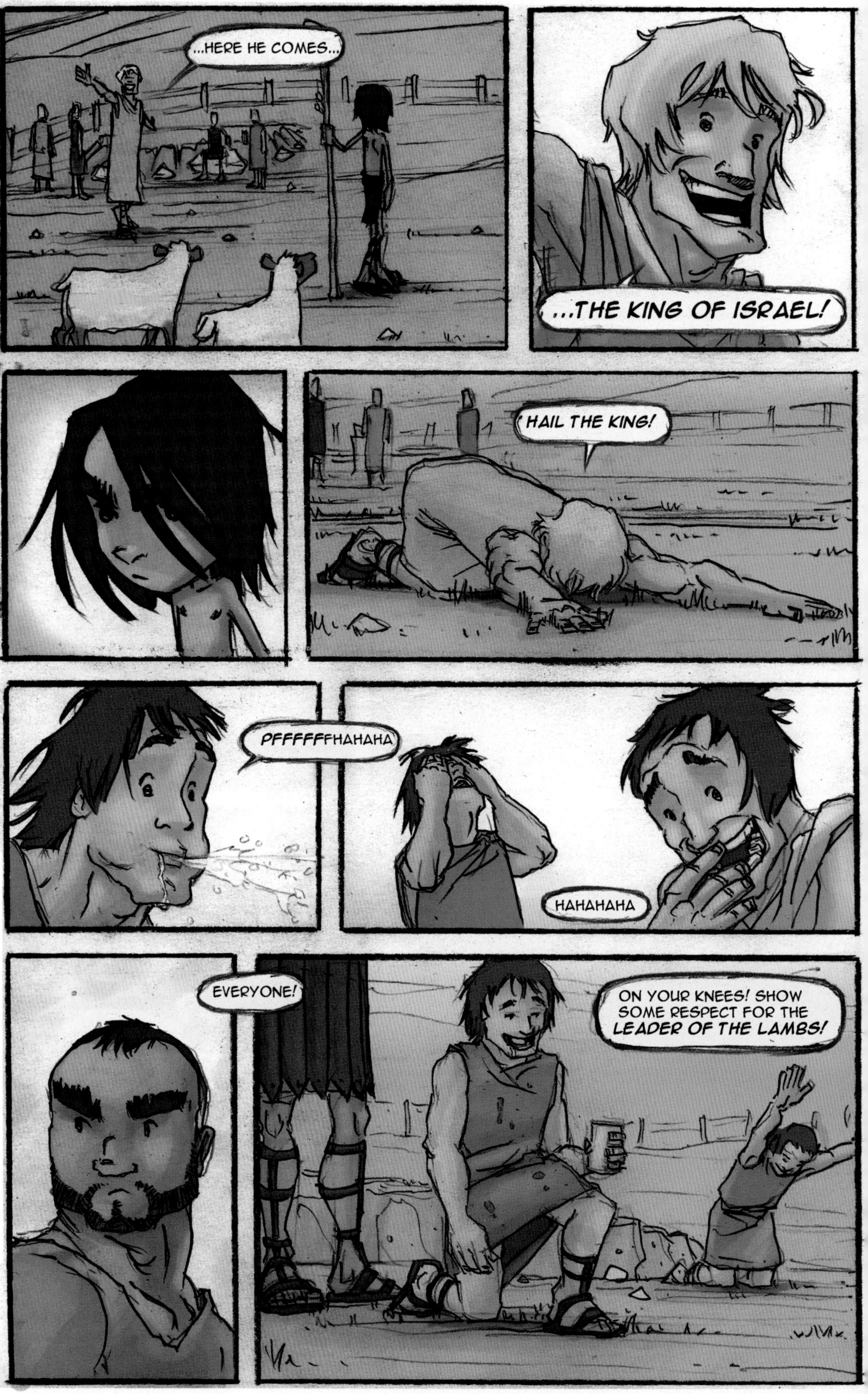
...HERE HE COMES...
...THE KING OF ISRAEL!
HAIL THE KING!
PFFFFFFHAHAHA
HAHAHAHA
EVERYONE!
ON YOUR KNEES! SHOW SOME RESPECT FOR THE LEADER OF THE LAMBS!

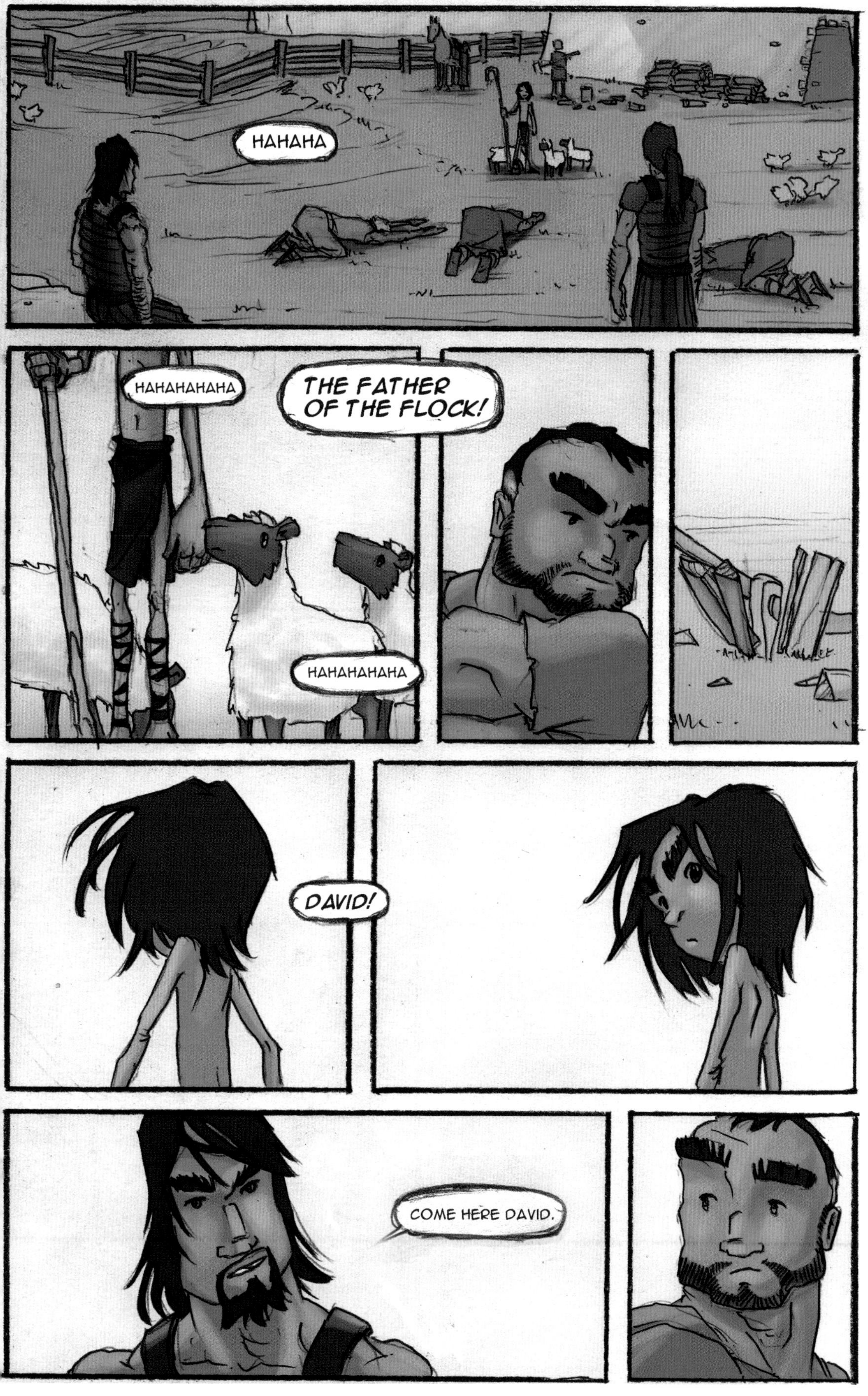
HAHAHA
HAHAHAHAHA
THE FATHER OF THE FLOCK!
HAHAHAHAHA
DAVID!
COME HERE DAVID.

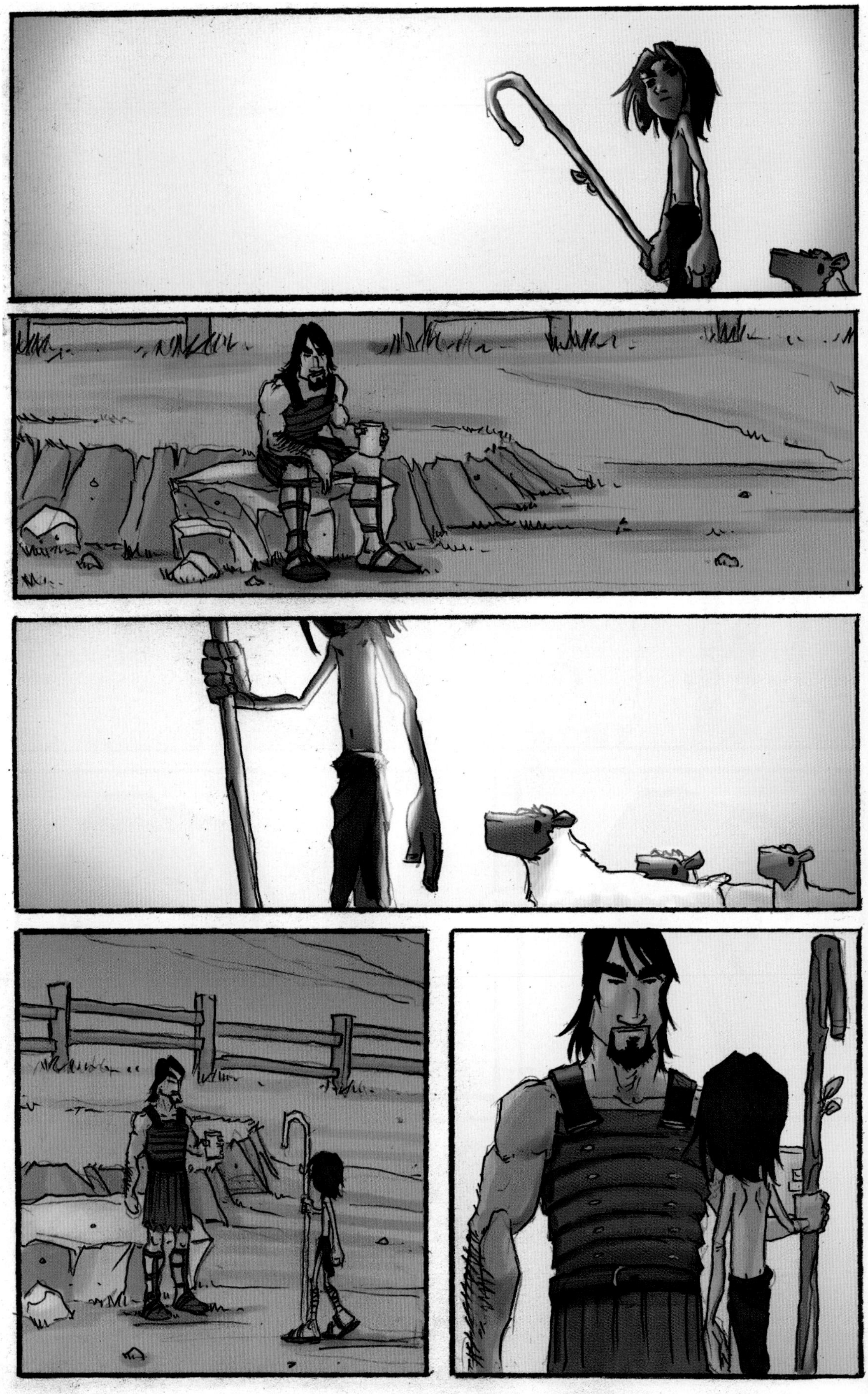

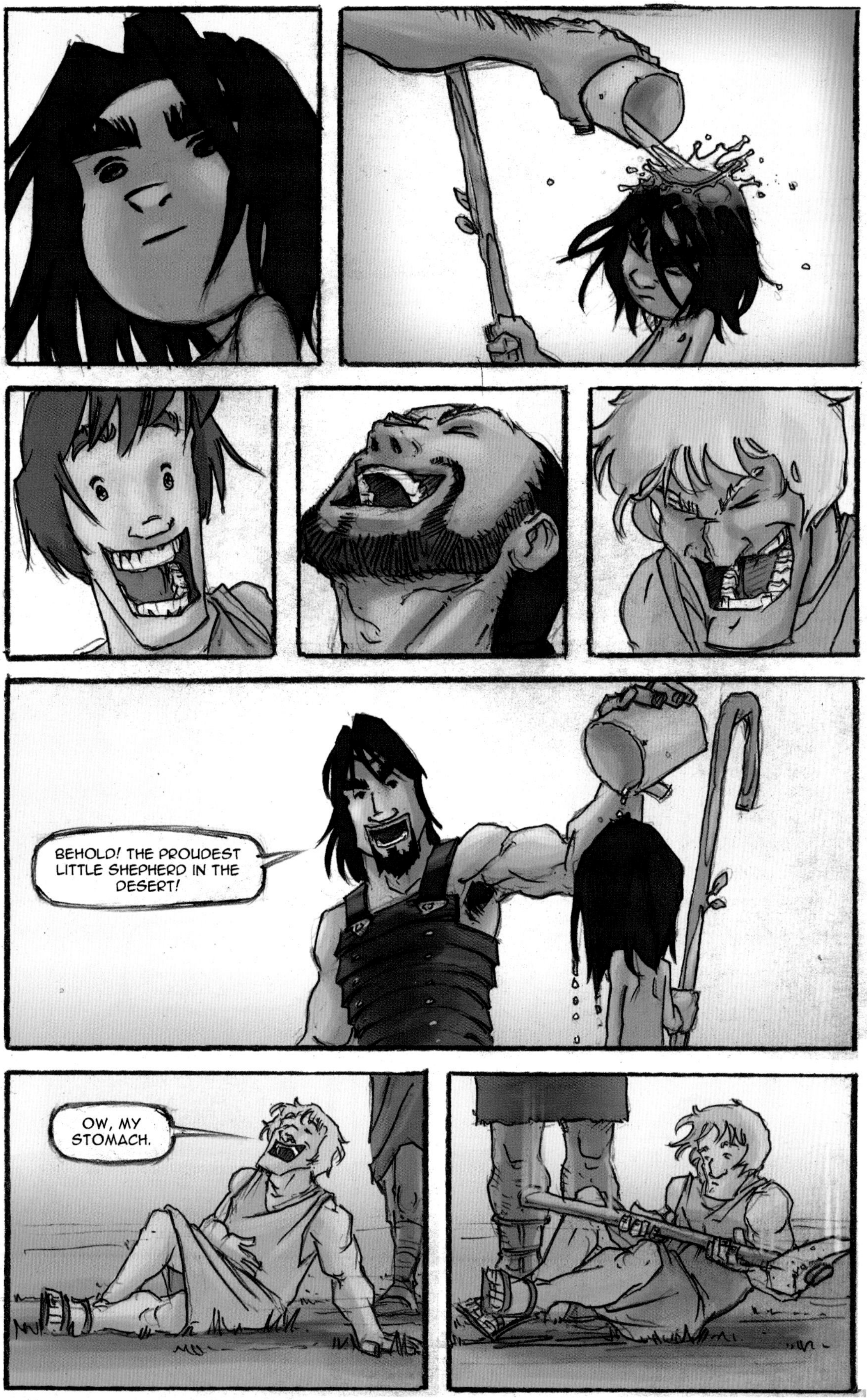
BEHOLD! THE PROUDEST LITTLE SHEPHERD IN THE DESERT!
OW, MY STOMACH.

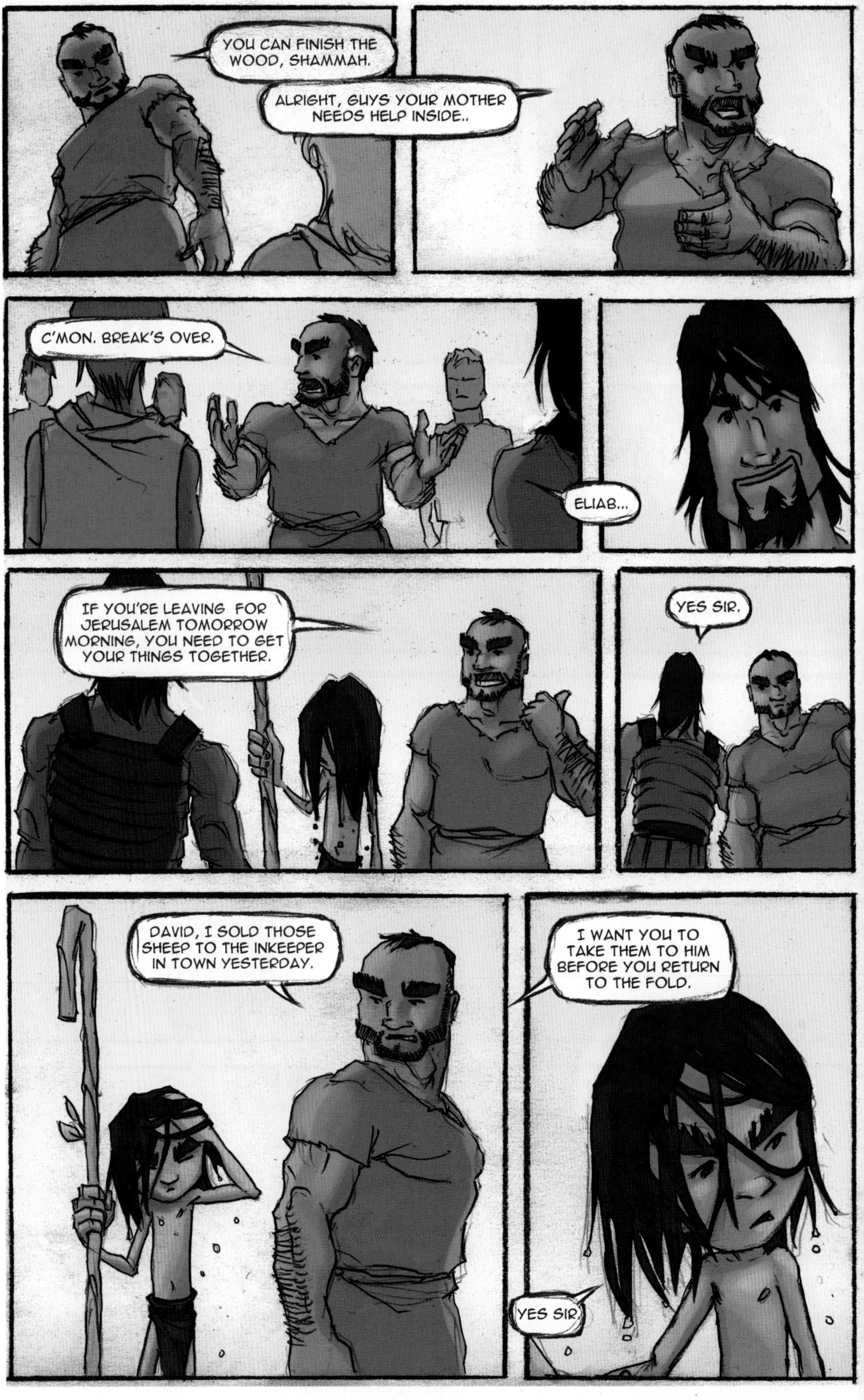
YOU CAN FINISH THE WOOD, SHAMMAH.
ALRIGHT, GUYS YOUR MOTHER NEEDS HELP INSIDE..
C'MON. BREAK'S OVER.
ELIAB...
IF YOU'RE LEAVING FOR JERUSALEM TOMORROW MORNING, YOU NEED TO GET YOUR THINGS TOGETHER.
YES SIR.
DAVID, I SOLD THOSE SHEEP TO THE INKEEPER IN TOWN YESTERDAY.
I WANT YOU TO TAKE THEM TO HIM BEFORE YOU RETURN TO THE FOLD.
YES SIR.

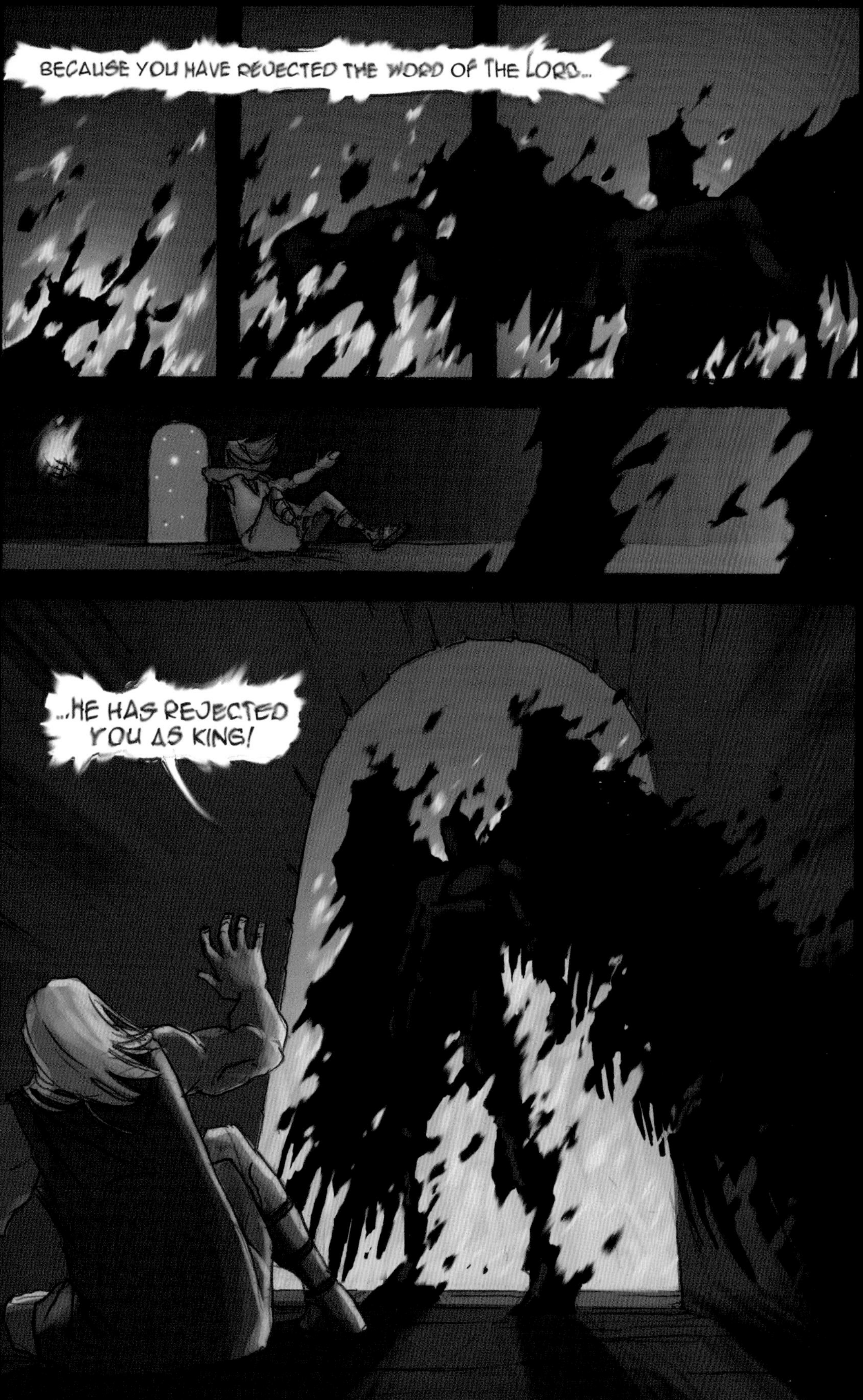
BECAUSE YOU HAVE REJECTED THE WORD OF THE LORD...
...HE HAS REJECTED YOU AS KING!

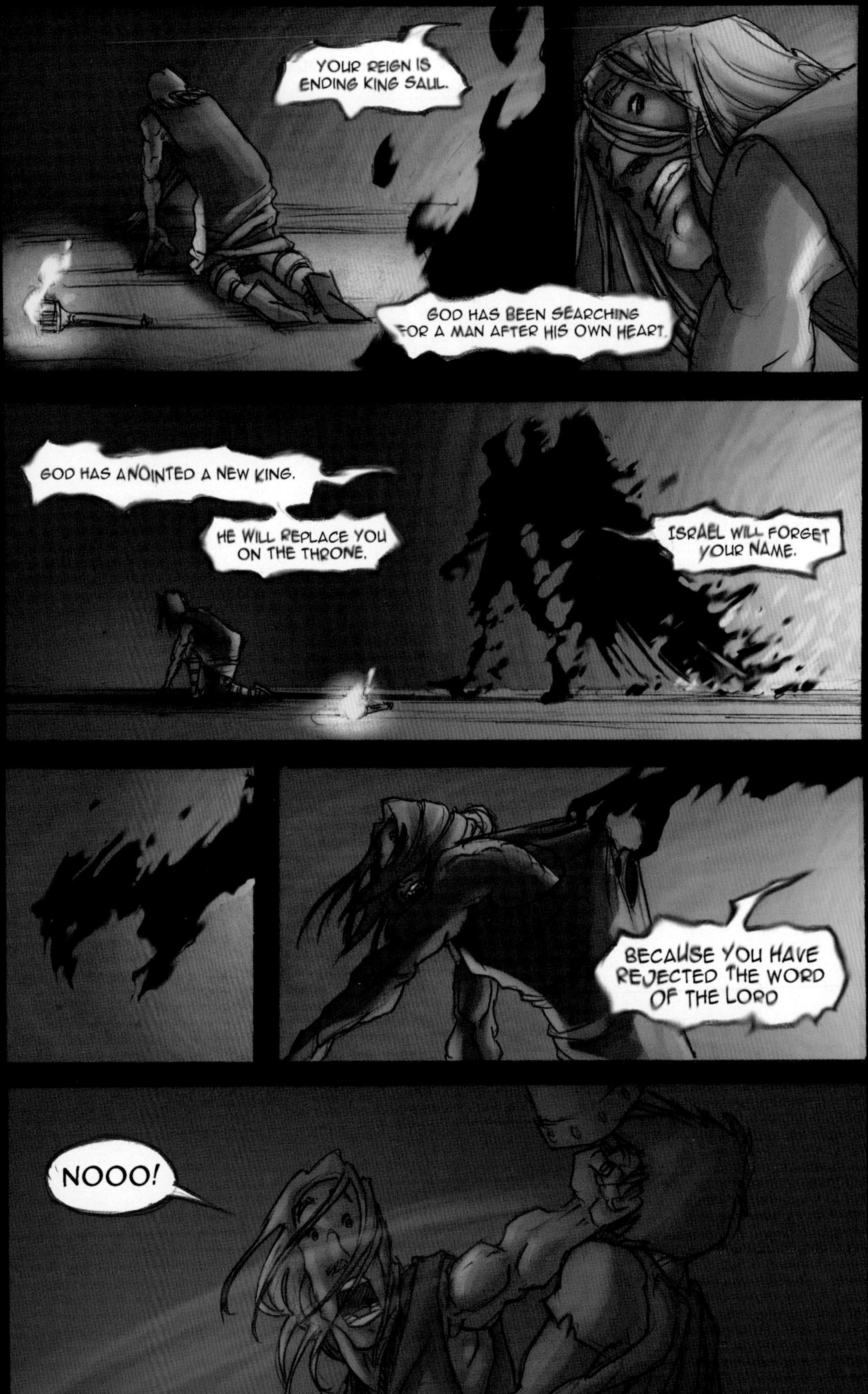

YOUR REIGN IS ENDING KING SAUL.
GOD HAS BEEN SEARCHING FOR A MAN AFTER HIS OWN HEART.
GOD HAS ANOINTED A NEW KING.
HE WILL REPLACE YOU ON THE THRONE.
ISRAEL WILL FORGET YOUR NAME.
BECAUSE YOU HAVE REJECTED THE WORD OF THE LORD
NOOO!

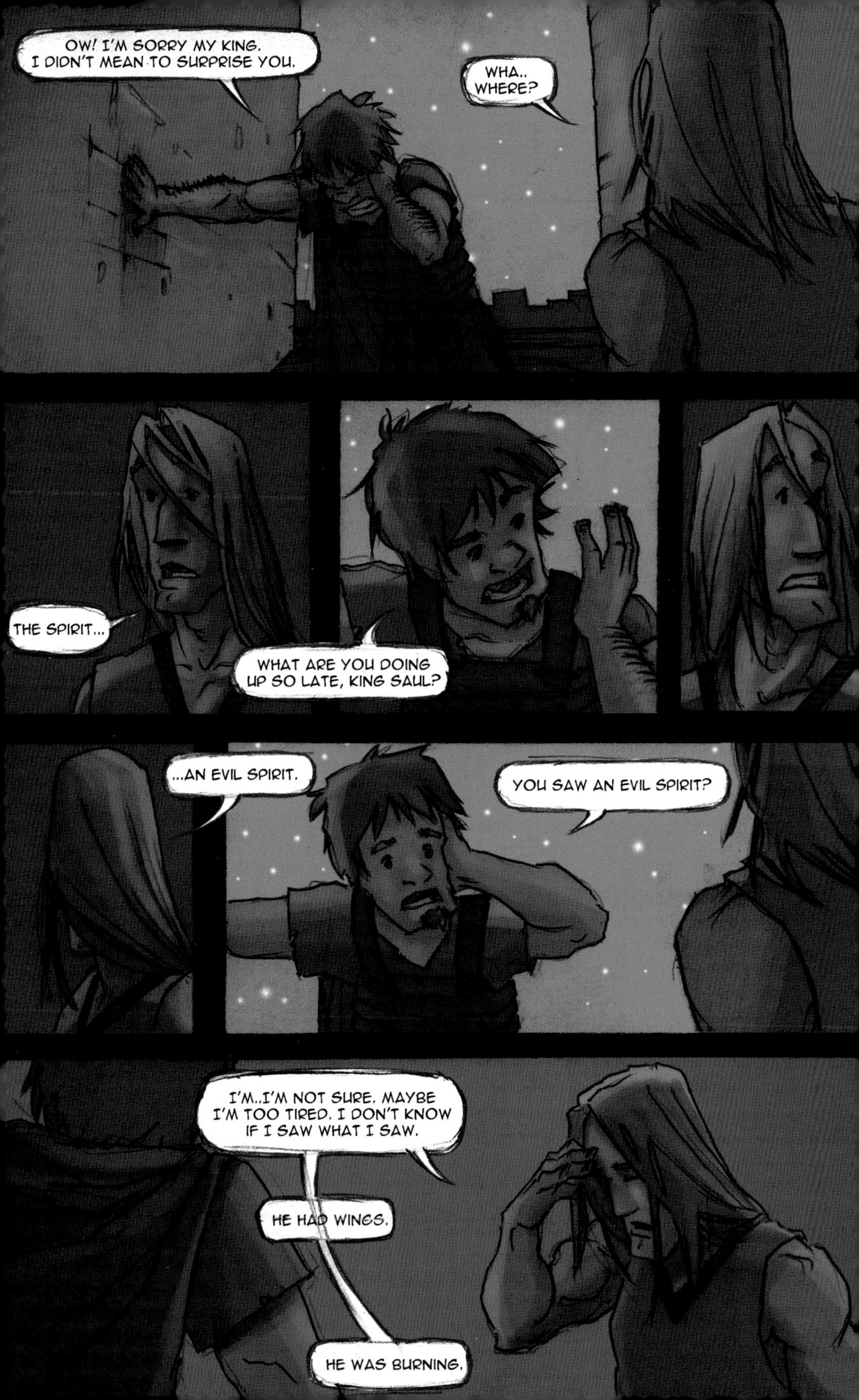
OW! I'M SORRY MY KING. I DIDN'T MEAN TO SURPRISE YOU.
WHA.. WHERE?
THE SPIRIT...
WHAT ARE YOU DOING UP SO LATE, KING SAUL?
...AN EVIL SPIRIT.
YOU SAW AN EVIL SPIRIT?
I'M..I'M NOT SURE. MAYBE I'M TOO TIRED. I DON'T KNOW IF I SAW WHAT I SAW.
HE HAD WINGS.
HE WAS BURNING.

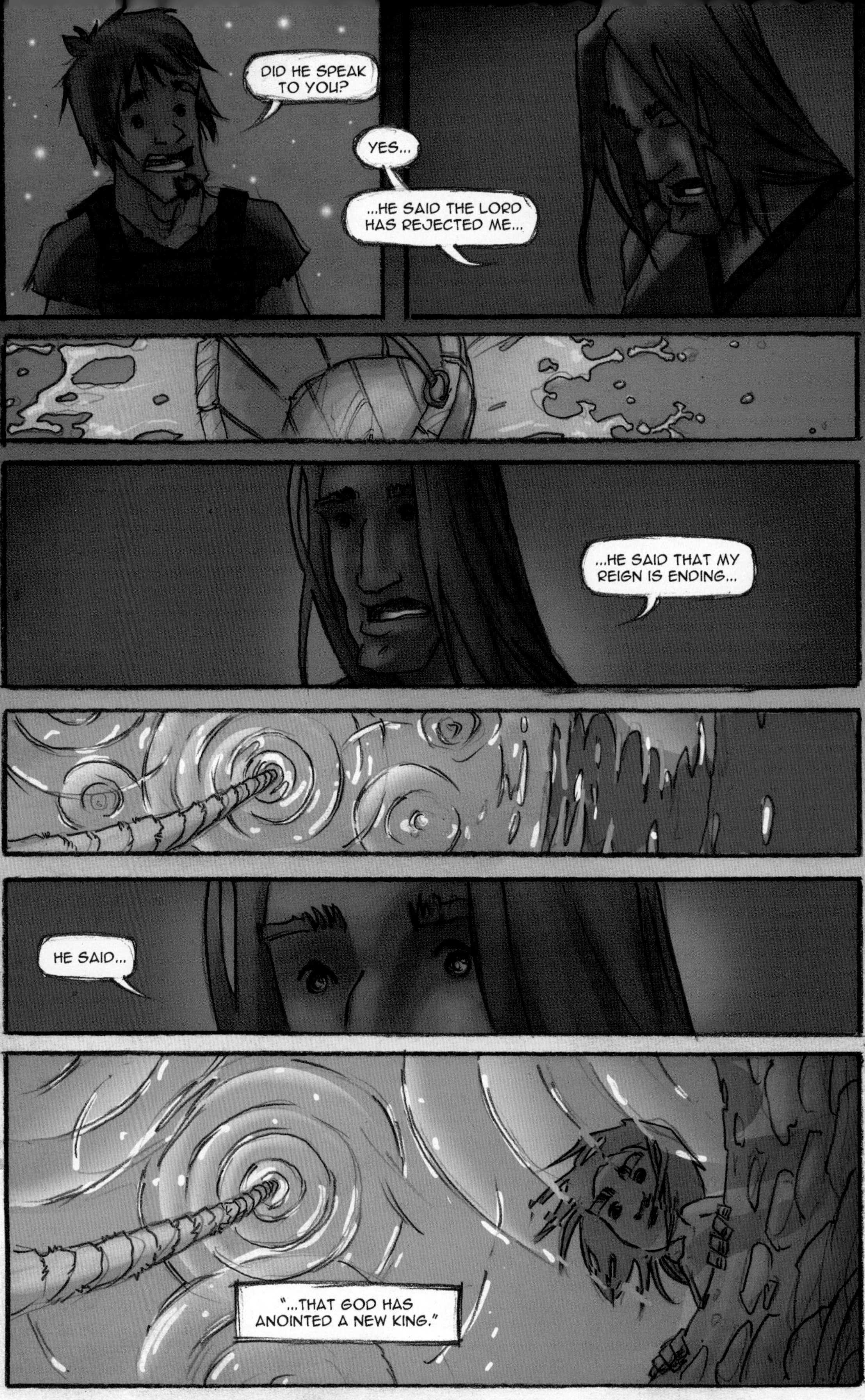
DID HE SPEAK TO YOU?
YES...
...HE SAID THE LORD HAS REJECTED ME...
...HE SAID THAT MY REIGN IS ENDING...
HE SAID...
"...THAT GOD HAS ANOINTED A NEW KING."

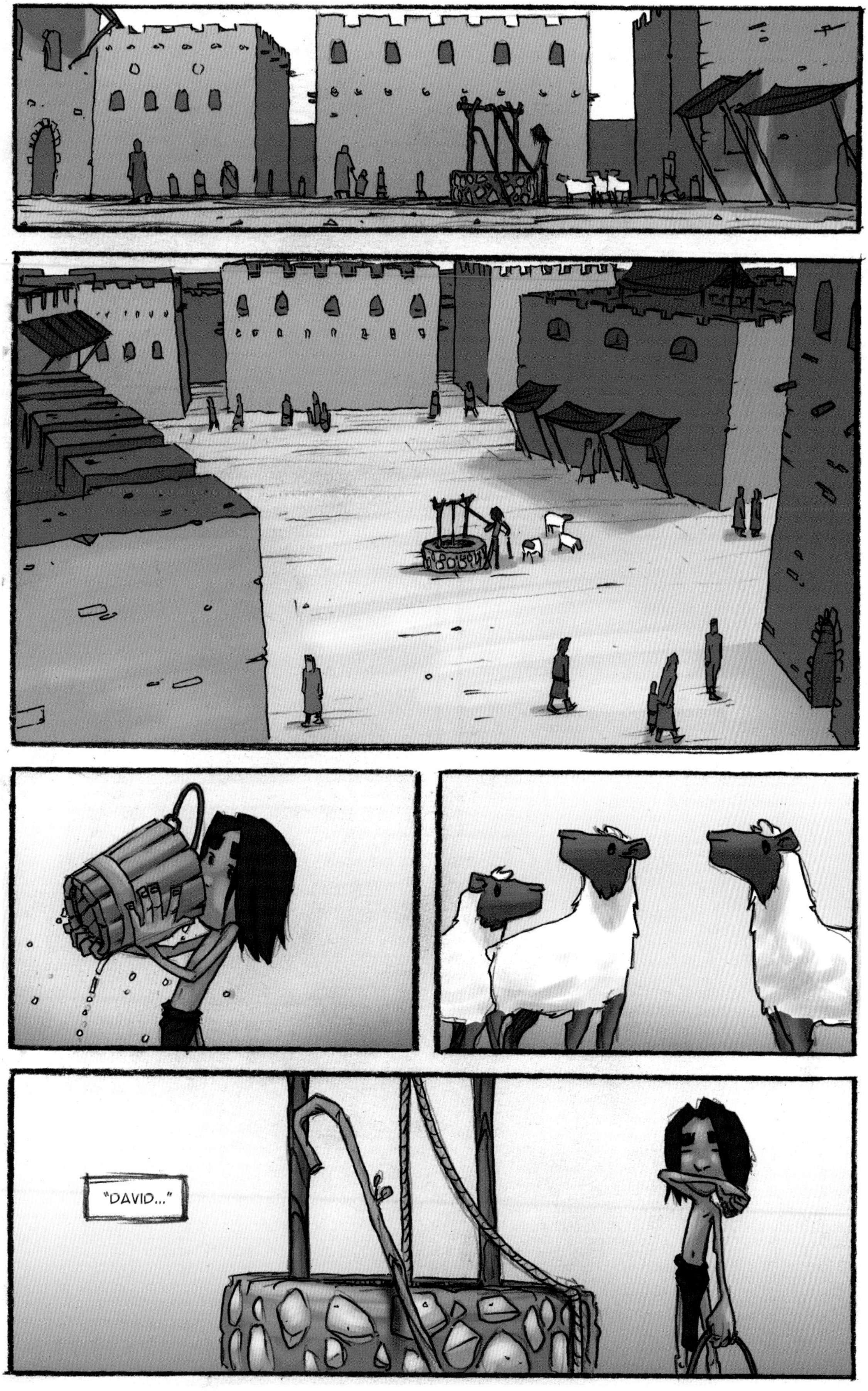
"DAVID..."

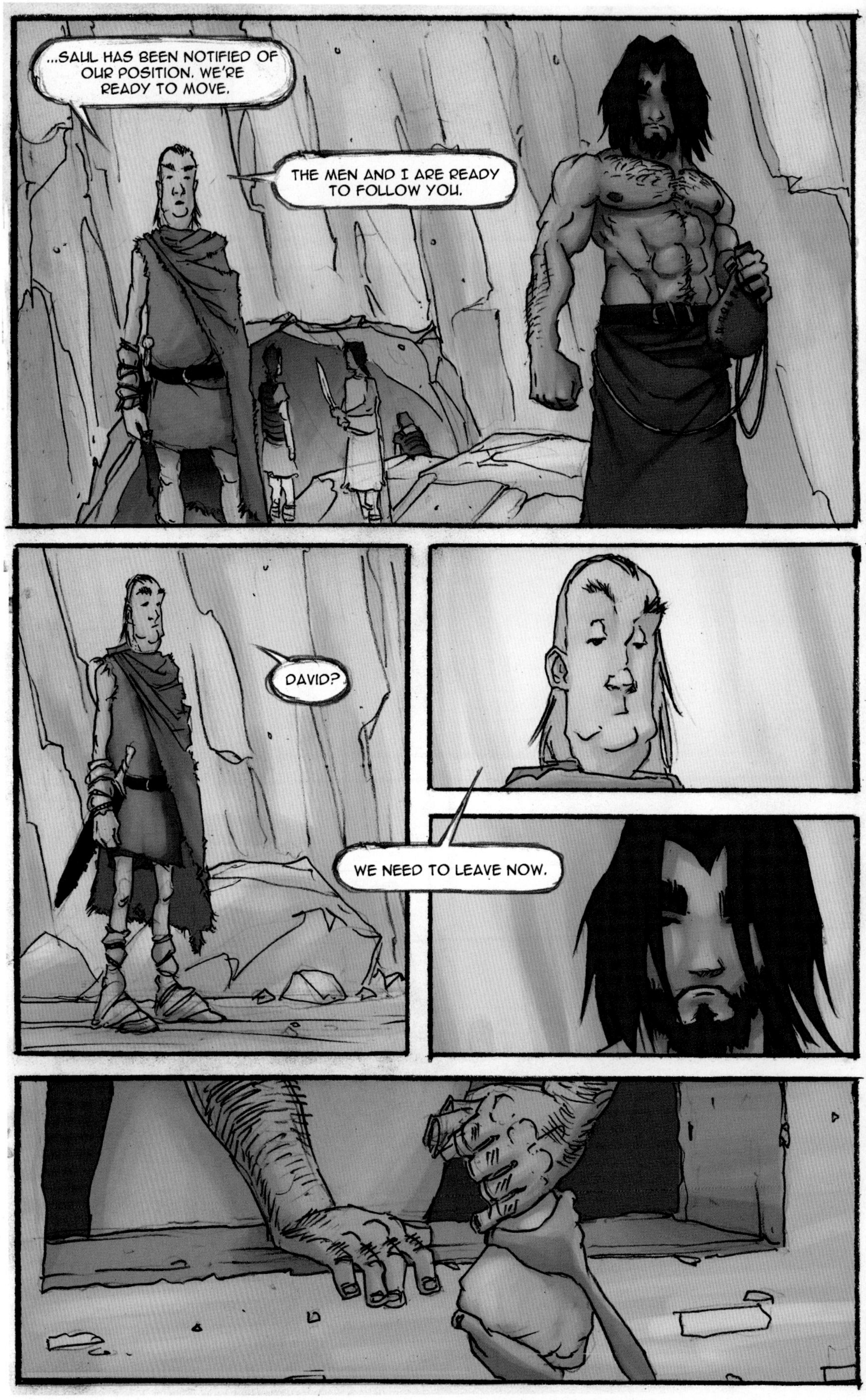
...SAUL HAS BEEN NOTIFIED OF OUR POSITION. WE'RE READY TO MOVE.
THE MEN AND I ARE READY TO FOLLOW YOU.
DAVID?
WE NEED TO LEAVE NOW.

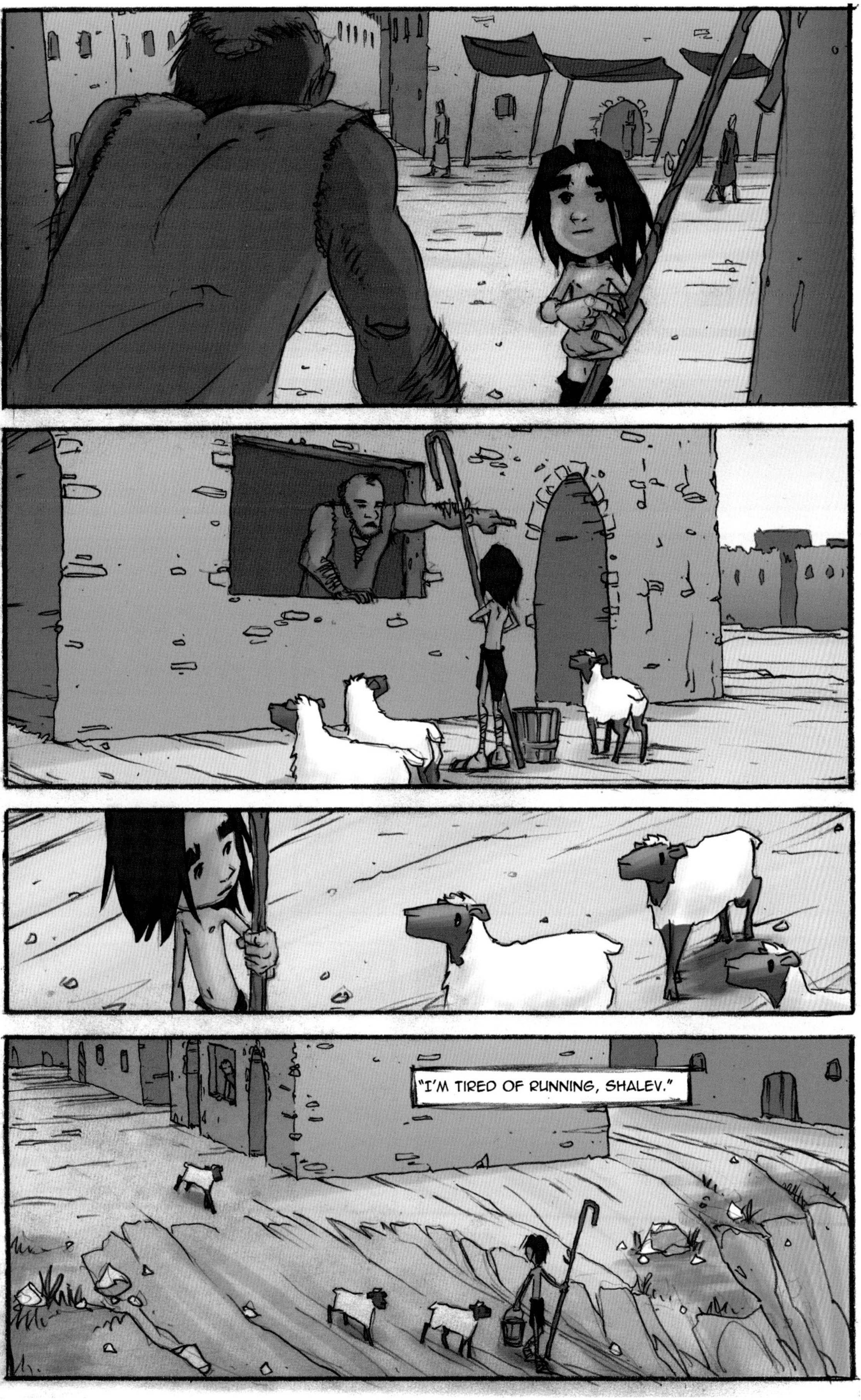
"I'M TIRED OF RUNNING, SHALEV."

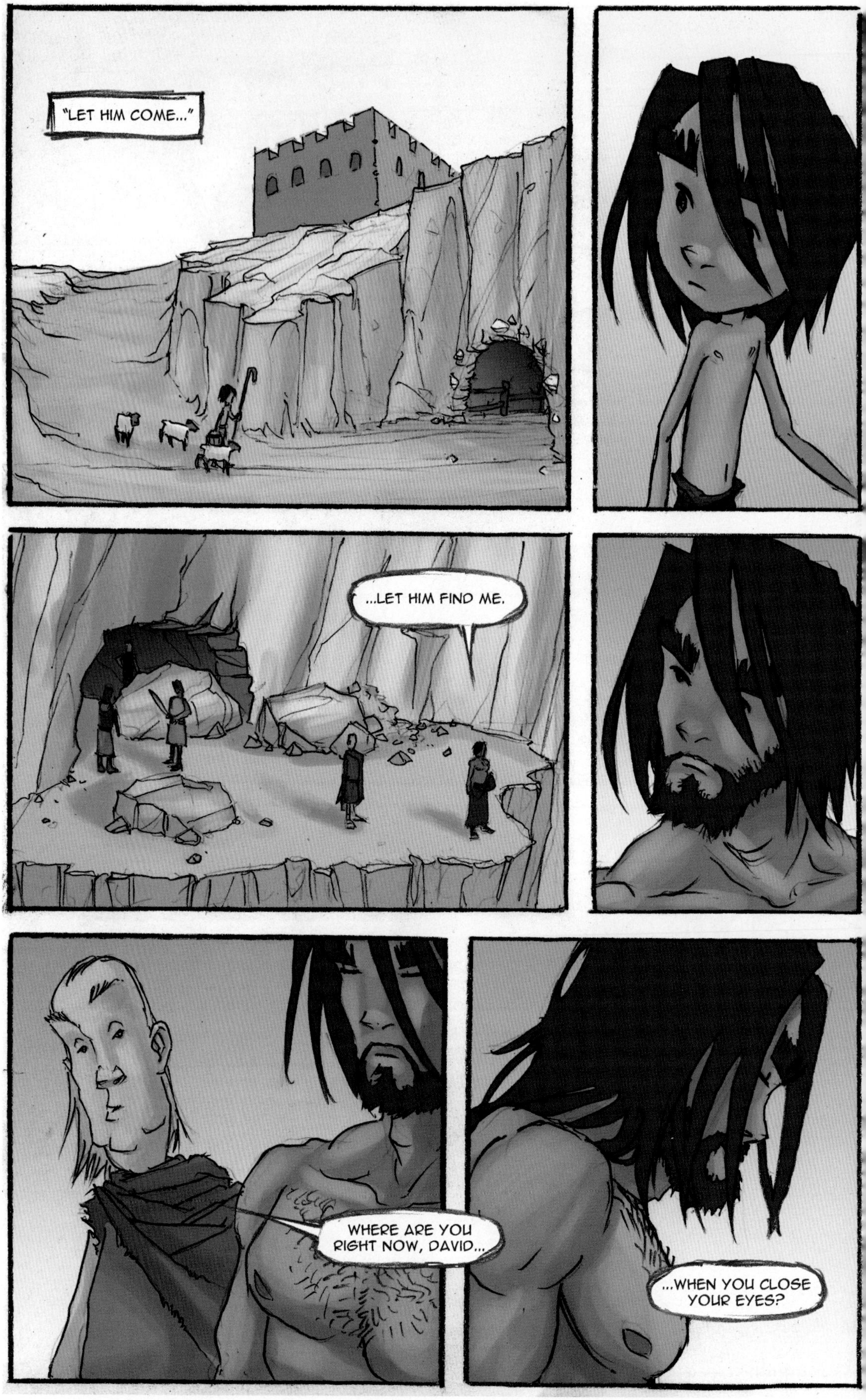
"LET HIM COME..."
...LET HIM FIND ME.
WHERE ARE YOU RIGHT NOW, DAVID...
...WHEN YOU CLOSE YOUR EYES?

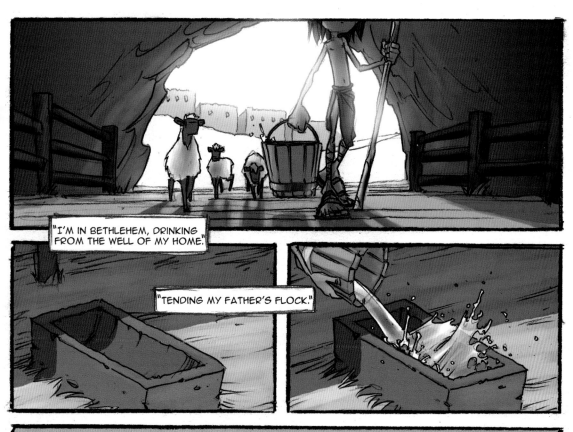

"I'M IN BETHLEHEM, DRINKING FROM THE WELL OF MY HOME."

"TENDING MY FATHER'S FLOCK."

WELL WHILE YOU'RE LOOKING INTO THE PAST, WHY DON'T YOU TELL ME AGAIN ABOUT THE DAY YOU WERE ANOINTED KING.

YOU'VE HEARD THE STORY BEFORE, SHALEV.

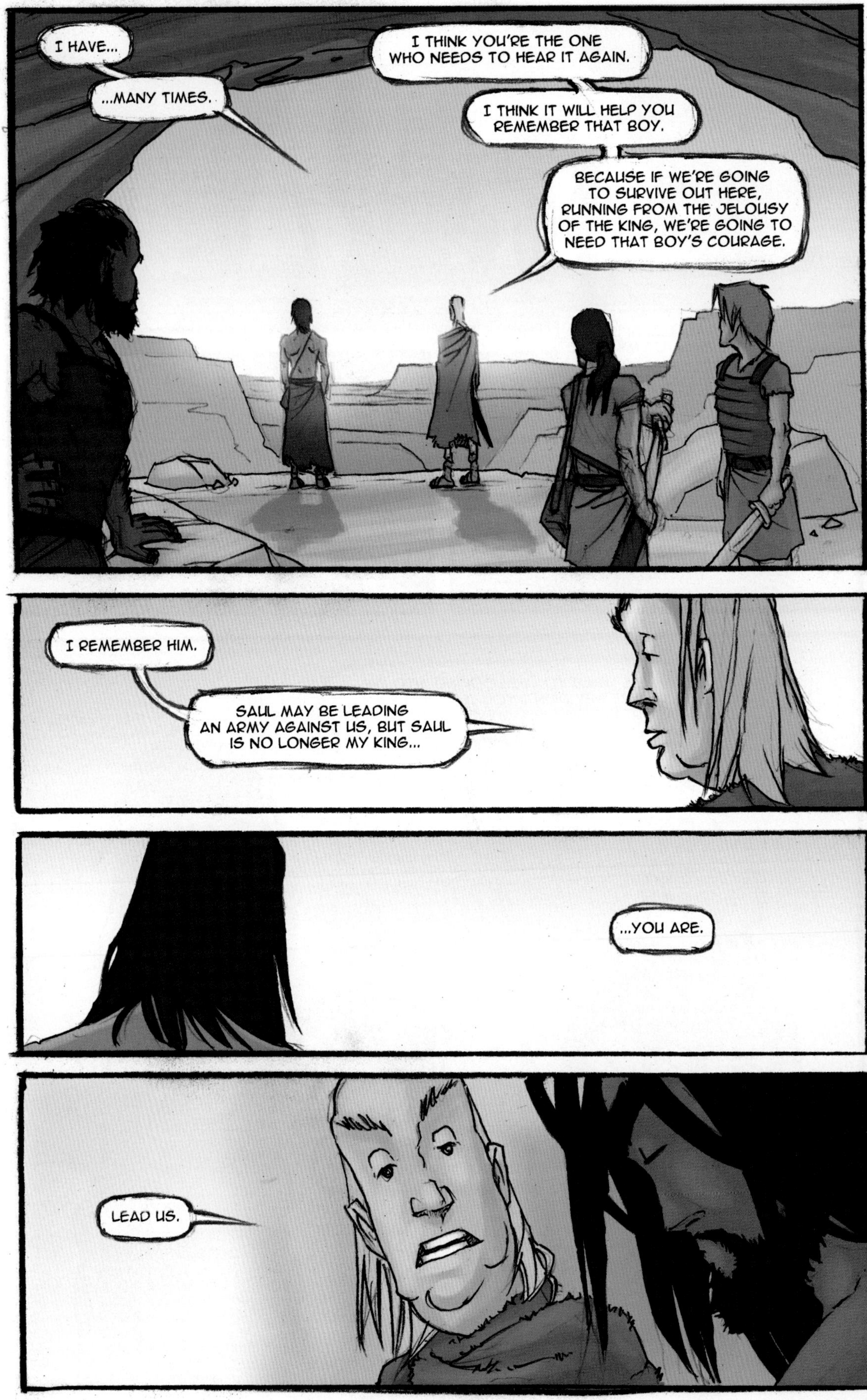
I HAVE...
...MANY TIMES.
I THINK YOU'RE THE ONE WHO NEEDS TO HEAR IT AGAIN.
I THINK IT WILL HELP YOU REMEMBER THAT BOY.
BECAUSE IF WE'RE GOING TO SURVIVE OUT HERE, RUNNING FROM THE JELOUSY OF THE KING, WE'RE GOING TO NEED THAT BOY'S COURAGE.
I REMEMBER HIM.
SAUL MAY BE LEADING AN ARMY AGAINST US, BUT SAUL IS NO LONGER MY KING...
...YOU ARE.
LEAD US.

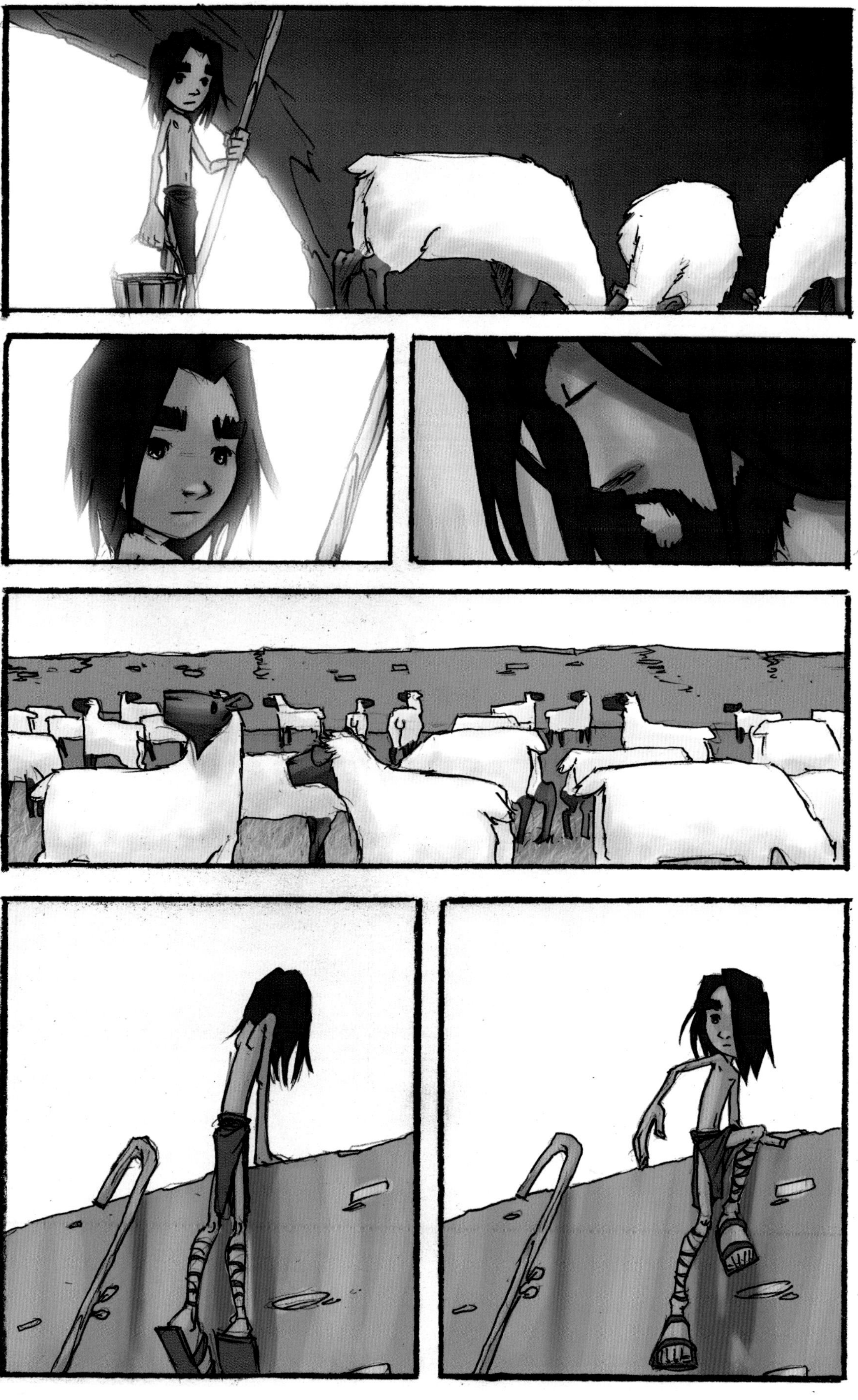

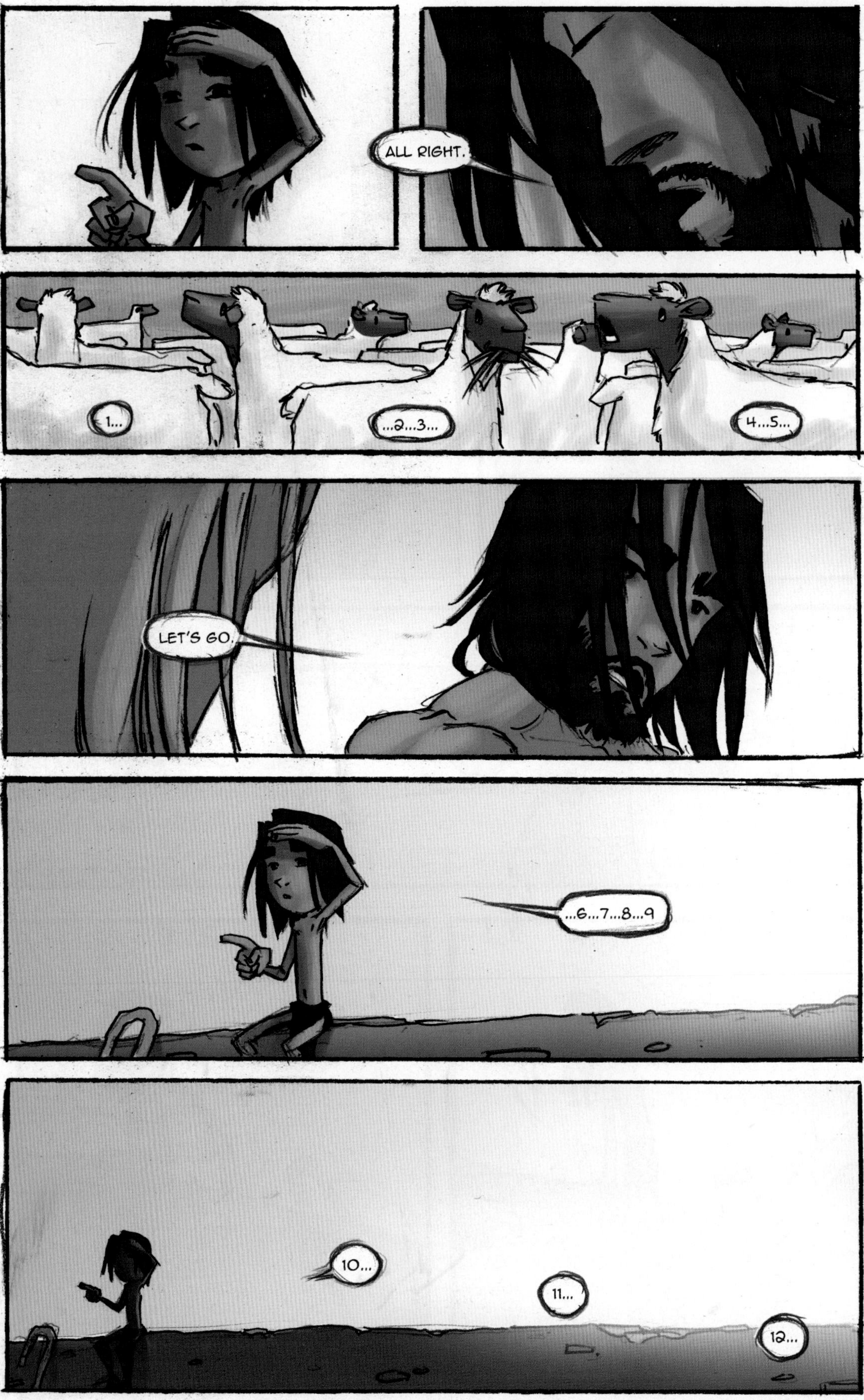
ALL RIGHT.
1...
...2...3...
4...5...
LET'S GO.
...6...7...8...9
10...
11...
12...